CHOPIN

AN INDEX OF HIS WORKS

CHOPIN

AN INDEX OF HIS WORKS
IN CHRONOLOGICAL ORDER

BY

MAURICE J. E. BROWN

LONDON
MACMILLAN & CO LTD
NEW YORK · ST MARTIN'S PRESS
1960

MACMILLAN AND COMPANY LIMITED
London Bombay Calcutta Madras Melbourne

THE MACMILLAN COMPANY OF CANADA LIMITED
Toronto

ST MARTIN'S PRESS INC
New York

PRINTED IN GREAT BRITAIN

CONTENTS

To
ARTHUR HEDLEY

FOREWORD

THIS book has been written to fill a gap in the Chopin literature. There is no lack, in fact there is a superfluity, of books dealing with the aesthetic appreciation of the works of the Polish composer, and with the interpretation of his works; there are several good, albeit incomplete, biographies of the man; there is one outstanding book containing full details of the bibliographical literature, by Bronisław Sydow. But of books devoted to a basic survey of Chopin's works, in chronological order, providing all known details of composition and publication, there is none.

I have gone to original sources, wherever possible, to obtain these details. The only reason why I have not produced the discovered information with the title of 'Thematic Catalogue' is that I have no wish to suggest that Chopin's compositions stand in any need of a catalogue number, and certainly no desire that each of his works should be labelled with an initial and a number, as those of Mozart and Schubert have been. In their cases it is essential, and the Köchel and Deutsch numbers supply a vital need. Chopin's opus numbers are a quite reliable guide to chronology, and are, in themselves, perfectly adequate for identification purposes.

But for the student, performer or critic of Chopin, to say nothing of the librarian, bookseller or collector, there is no ready means of reference to his individual works. The Index to be found in the following pages not only presents a survey of his works, chronologically set out, but also provides a ready and instantly obtained series of essential facts about each work.

These facts embody the dates and places of composition; the date of publication of all the first editions (in the case of his mature works that means of the French, English and German editions); points of interest or importance about the composition, publication or first performance of each work; and, finally, the whereabouts, if it is known, of the existing manuscripts.[1]

There are many reasons why such a book as this Index has not hitherto been written. Chopin's background includes Poland, Austria and Germany, France, and, to a certain degree, England—or perhaps 'Britain' would be more accurate! The number of musicologists who can command Polish, German, French and English must be rather limited, and without all four of these languages, Chopin research cannot be as thorough-going as it should be. Imperfections in this Index are due to my own elementary knowledge of Polish, and I have had either to use translations of Polish documents into German, or to rely on my own imperfect reading of the originals. Nevertheless, to wait until someone with a command of all four of these languages, together with the necessary musical knowledge, and a love for Chopin's music, *does* emerge, and undertakes the necessary sifting, might be to wait for a very long time, and however faulty the Index may be, it does, at least, make an effort to get the necessary studies started.

Another reason why this kind of book has not been compiled before, and which adds to the difficulties of a compiler today, is that Chopin seems not to have aroused the interest of bibliographers, particularly the industrious German bibliographers of the nineteenth century, in the same degree as the great German composers have done. The bibliographical source material for Chopin is considerably smaller than that for other composers, of a comparable standing. It is a surprising fact that whereas large, and sometimes complete, collections of the first editions of all the great composers can be found, not only in the larger national libraries of the world, but even in private possession,

---

[1] The final section in each item, entitled 'MS.' or 'MSS.' gives the whereabouts of *autograph* manuscripts. If, in this section, there are references to copies, made by other hands, this is made clear in every case.

this is certainly not the case with Chopin. To give two examples: the British Museum possesses only an incomplete set of Wessel's English edition of Chopin, and the collection of French first editions of Chopin in the Bibliothèque Nationale, Paris, lacks several examples.

There are, of course, large collections of these first editions in private possession in Europe: for example, that of Mr. Antony van Hoboken, Ascona, and that of Mr. Arthur Hedley, London. But these two collections are not complete, and in some cases, after a vain search extending far and wide, I have begun to wonder if a single copy of some of Chopin's first editions, e.g. of Chabal's publication of the 'Emil Gaillard' Mazurka, or of Kauffmann's publication of the E minor Waltz, is still extant anywhere in the world! The unhappy experiences of Poland, in two World Wars, have also led to the destruction of many such copies, as well as to the loss of autograph manuscripts.

The following list gives the more important catalogues of Chopin's works, which appeared between 1845 or so and 1954. Many of them are in order of opus numbers. The earlier ones are, understandably, incomplete and inaccurate, and the later ones, either by reason of brevity, or because of subsequent discoveries, similarly unreliable. Mr. Hedley's two catalogues are, it goes without saying, excellent, but in both of them reasons of space lead to the omission of full details, and neither of them, as he would doubtless admit, aims at completeness.

1. MS. Thematic Catalogue prepared for Jane Stirling by Chopin and Auguste Franchomme *c.* 1845. Later additions (by Sigismond von Neukomm?) continue the list to Op. 73, and beyond. Chopin wrote in his own hand Opp. 1, 37, 38, 48–50, 57 and 58. Only the first item is given for the sets of Studies in Opp. 10 and 25, and for the set of Preludes, Op. 28. The MS., which bears Jane Stirling's authentification, was reproduced in facsimile as a frontispiece to the *Oxford Edition of Chopin's Works*, vol. I, London, 1932.
2. *Thematisches Verzeichniss der im Druck erschienenen Kompositionen von*

Fr. Chopin. Breitkopf & Haertel, Leipzig, October 1852. Later issues, with additions, till *c.* 1870.

3. MS. List of the then unpublished works, prepared by Chopin's sister Louise (Ludwica), *c.* 1853 (probably for Fontana's projected publication of the posthumous works). Louise died in 1855, but someone else in the family, her sister Isabella or her daughter of the same name, added details—date, publisher, etc.—to the items as they were published. This list, known in the Index as 'Louise's list', was published for the first time in *Souvenirs inédits de Chopin,* 1904 (see Appendix IX).

4. *Thematisches Verzeichniss der in Deutschland erschienenen Instrumental = Kompositionen von Friedrich Chopin mit Beifugüng der Textanfänge seiner Lieder,* Dr. Oscar Paul. It was a supplement to the *Musikalisches Wochenblatt* of 4 January 1870, published by Ernst Wilhelm Fritzsch, Leipzig.

5. *Thematisches Verzeichniss der im Druck erschienenen Kompositionen von Fr. Chopin.* Enlarged and revised. Breitkopf & Haertel, Leipzig, 1888.

6. *Stufenweise geordnete Verzeichniss sammtlicher Kompositionen von Fr. Chopin,* Dr. Hans Schmidt, Professor at the Conservatoire, Vienna. Later incorporated into the 1888 Catalogue above.

7. *Frederick Chopin as a man and musician,* Frederick Niecks, London 1888, vol. II.

8. *A Handbook to Chopin's Works,* C. Ashton Jonson. Wm. Reeves, London, 1905. Revised edition, 1908.

9. *Chopin,* Arthur Hedley, pages 187–193. J. M. Dent & Sons, London, 1946.

10. *Bibliografia F. F. Chopina,* Bronisław Edward Sydow, Warsaw, 1949

11. *Almanach Chopinowski 1949,* Sydow, Warsaw, 1950.

12. 'Chopin', Arthur Hedley, in *Grove's Dictionary,* 5th Edition. Macmillan, London, 1954.

For each work in the Index I have quoted, in brackets, after the particular publisher, the Publisher's Number (P.N.) of the first edition. These numbers, treated with care, constitute, in the words of Dr. Otto Erich Deutsch, a 'new tool of bibliography', but it is a two-edged tool, and can hardly ever be relied on, in isolation, for the purpose of dating a publication. In the case of Wessel, for example, it is clear that a whole batch of Publisher's Numbers was allotted to Chopin, to be used as, and when, Wessel acquired a new composition by him. Consecutive numbers, in Wessel's case, may indicate publications separated by several years.[1] In the same way, delayed publication of a work from Breitkopf & Haertel renders their Publisher's Number useless; contemporary advertisements are then the only reliable source of information.

It is by the aid of such advertisements that I have, in nearly all cases, obtained precise details of publication dates. In France and Germany an unbroken sequence of advertisements, in this or that periodical, enables one to do so with accuracy; in England, the lack of any musical periodical in the crucial years 1833–1835 makes the task more difficult, but here the two bibliographical aids, Wessel's Publisher's Number and the acquisition dates on the first editions in the British Museum, taken in conjunction, help to bridge the gap. The famous *Verzeichniss der Musikalien* of Hofmeister is useful for the German and Polish editions, although even this was not published during the essential years 1839–1844. Senff, of Leipzig, however, issued a *Jahrbuch für Musik*, containing publications from Germany, Austria and Poland, between 1842 and 1852.

The eight posthumous works, Opp. 66 to 73, appeared in Berlin and Paris during 1855–1856. They were edited—and that word has here some of its slightly less desirable undertones—by Chopin's friend Julian Fontana. He obtained permission on 16 July 1853 from Chopin's family in Warsaw, that is, from his widowed mother Justina, and his sisters Louise Jedrzejewicz and Isabella Barcińska, to publish these works. They accordingly appeared under the title 'Oeuvres posthumes pour le piano de Fréd. Chopin publiés sur manuscrits originaux avec autorisation de sa famille par Jules Fontana'. He arranged them rather arbitrarily in categories, so that early mazurkas and waltzes jostle with late ones, and wrote an uninformative preface, dated May 1855, introducing his edition. The eight sets of works were published in Berlin, by A. M. Schlesinger, with the opus numbers as we know them, and in Paris, by J. Meissonnier

---

[1] See *Music and Letters*, London, October 1958.

fils, without opus numbers. Fontana's prolonged negotiations with Breitkopf & Haertel of Leipzig had come to nothing: it is worth mention that the Leipzig firm refused to publish these posthumous works on the grounds of their inferiority! They did not appear in London, until many years had passed, although their copyright was registered at Stationer's Hall in 1855. Both the French and German editions contained a portrait of Chopin by Ary Scheffer (1795–1858) as a frontispiece, in Paris engraved by Raunhim, in Berlin by Waldow. The final opus number, Op. 74, comprising the sixteen (later seventeen) Polish songs appeared two years later, in 1857, and then only in Germany.

The three editions of Chopin's works, published during his lifetime in France, England and Germany, sometimes give references to publishers in other countries, in Italy, Belgium, Poland, Russia and so forth: these references have been omitted from the Index whenever it was felt that the firms specified were those only of agencies for the main editions, and not actual publishers of the work concerned. Nor has it been possible to give details of all the re-publication during Chopin's lifetime of collections of his works in similar forms, e.g. 'Complete Polonaises' or 'Complete Impromptus'. In most cases the publisher merely bound together the separate issues, or re-used the original plates giving the set a new title-page, and the pieces a consecutive numbering.

The various appendixes at the end of this book attempt to give the Chopin student, in a concise and readily available form, certain factual details which may be necessary to him, and to find which would entail a good deal of page-turning in the biographies. In one case, that of the appendix devoted to the poets of the songs, the information given is not particularly important, but, as far as I know, appears nowhere else. Wessel's English edition is listed in full, partly because the Index is primarily addressed to readers of English, and partly because his numbering of the works does not follow the opus numbers. The Bibliography is not intended to be a complete one: I have included in it only such works as I consider significant, and relevant, to this annotated Index.

Many people have helped me with the details of this book. I cannot hope to mention them all individually for the list runs to well over a hundred names. Chiefly I am indebted to Mr. Arthur Hedley, the eminent Chopin scholar, whose collection of Chopiniana is unrivalled in the world. To Mr. Antony van Hoboken I am almost as deeply indebted for the many details of importance from his fine collection of Chopin first editions. The third of my major helpers is Mlle. Simone Wallon, Assistant Librarian at the Conservatoire de Musique, Bibliothèque Nationale, Paris; I am most grateful for her valuable help in connection with the collection of Chopin MSS. and first editions in that library. Other librarians to whom my thanks are due are Mlle. B. Monkiewicz, of the Bibliothèque Polonaise, Paris; Herr Dr. F. Grasberger, of the Nationalbibliothek, Vienna; and Mrs. Hilda Andrews, of the Polish Cultural Institute, London. Amongst other people, who have made the preparation of this book possible, I should like especially to thank Mlles. Suzanne and Denise Chainaye, the well-known French authorities on Chopin; Dr. Otto Erich Deutsch of Vienna; Mr. Adam Harasowski, the authority on Polish folk-song; Mr. Adam Rieger, editor of *Ruch Muzyczny*, Cracow; and, finally, M. Alfred Cortot, Lausanne, whose kindness in providing details of the Chopin MSS. in his possession is, alas, not too common amongst such fortunate possessors.

In conclusion—an appeal to any users of this book: I stress once again my realisation that the Index has many imperfections and many gaps, inevitable in such a pioneering effort. If its readers can supply any of these deficiencies, I should be grateful to hear of them.

M.J.E.B.

POLONAISE in G minor. 1817

Publication:

> J. J. Cybulski, Warsaw (Nr. 1882). November 1817.
> Republished in 1927 (see below).

Dedicated to Mlle. la Comtesse Viktoire Skarbek, daughter of Count Frederick Skarbek. Count Skarbek was a pupil of Nicolas Chopin, the composer's father.

The Polonaise, twenty-two bars long, with a sixteen-bar Trio in B flat major, was reviewed in a Warsaw literary periodical, *Pamiętnik Warszawski*, of January 1818, amongst a list of Polish books published in 1817. This review was known, but all trace of the music had disappeared. In 1924 a copy of it was found by Zdisław Jachimecki of Cracow. He found it in some bound copies of piano pieces which had been published in Warsaw between 1816 and 1830. The four volumes of these bound pieces had belonged to the poet Josef Gatuszka of Cracow. The copy of the Polonaise had been inscribed by Chopin himself 'Jan Białobłocki, writer'. A second copy was in the possession of Laura Ciechomska (a descendant of Chopin's sister, Louise) of Warsaw, whose collection was destroyed in 1939. A third copy is now in the possession of Antony van Hoboken, Ascona, Switzerland.

Jachimecki announced his discovery and republished the piece, in facsimile, in various musical periodicals of Europe, including the *Monthly Musical Record*, London, March 1927. In 1947 he edited the Polonaise, together with the Polonaise in B flat (3) and the Polonaise in A flat (5) and the three were published as *Trzy Polonezy* ['Three Polonaises']: *1817–1821*, by S. A. Krzyanowski, Cracow.

The title-page of the Polonaise has been frequently reproduced in facsimile. The attribution is 'faite / par Frédéric Chopin / musicien âgé de huit ans /'.

(*a*) The 'Cracow' copy was reproduced in the *Monthly Musical Record*, March 1927. The words 'faite' and 'musicien' have been scratched out in this copy, possibly by Chopin himself.

(*b*) The 'Warsaw' copy was reproduced in Binental's *Documents*, Warsaw, 1930. It is unmarked in any way.

(*c*) On the 'Ascona' copy, only the word 'faite' is scratched out.

The Abbé Cybulski was the proprietor of a small music-printing business near St. Mary's Church, Warsaw. Biało-błocki (1805–1828) was a boarder in the Chopin household (see the note after **10** and also **17**).

MS. Lost.

2

MILITARY MARCH. 1817

Publication:

1817, without the composer's name. No copy of this publication is known.

The March won the approval of the Grand Duke Constantine and on his orders was scored for military band (not by the composer) and performed for him in 1817.

MS. Lost.

3

POLONAISE in B flat major. 1817

Publication:

(*a*) A facsimile reproduction in *Kuryer Literacko-Naukowy*, Cracow, 22 January 1934.

(*b*) A facsimile reproduction in the *Journal of the Frédéric Chopin Institute*, Warsaw, vol. I, no. 1, 1937. Both facsimiles edited by Zdisław Jachimecki.

The Polonaise, twenty bars long, with a sixteen-bar Trio in G minor, is known through a copy made by the composer's father, Nicolas, and inscribed: 'Polonaise pour le piano forte composée par F. Chopin âgé 8 ans'. The copy was one of the autographs belonging to Alexander Poliński of Warsaw, the noted collector and historian of Polish music. After his death it passed into the State Collection, Warsaw, but was destroyed during the Second World War.

The work was identified, as well as published, by Jachimecki; he also edited it for publication in 1947 as the second of 'Three Polonaises' (see 1).

MSS. (1) Lost.

(2) Nicolas Chopin's copy: destroyed.

Lost works of the period:

(*a*) A set of variations (mentioned in the *Pamiętnik Warszawski* of 1818.)

(*b*) Two Polish dances presented by Chopin to the Empress Maria Teoderowna, mother of the Czar, on the occasion of her visit to Warsaw on 26 September 1818. One of these may have been the previous item.

4

Mᴀᴢᴛᴜᴍᴀ ('Mᴀᴢᴜᴛᴇᴋ') in D major. (?) 1820

Publication:

A facsimile reproduction in the *Kuryer*, Warsaw, no. 51, 20 February 1910.

The piece, thirty-four bars long, was part of the collection of autograph manuscripts belonging to Alexander Poliński (see 3).

MS. Destroyed in the Second World War (formerly in the possession of the State Collection, Warsaw).

5

Pᴏᴸᴏɴᴀɪᴛᴇ in A flat major. April 1821

Publication:

> Gebethner & Wolff, Warsaw (2515). 1902. This was from an unsatisfactory transcript made by Jan Michałowski.
> *Die Musik*, Berlin (clean). October 1908.

Dedicated to Wojciech (=Adalbert) Zywny (1756–1842), Polish pianist and violinist, Chopin's first music master.

The Polonaise, twenty-six bars long, with a thirteen-bar Trio in E flat major, was performed for Zywny by Chopin on 23 April 1821. The manuscript, a doubtful autograph, was exhibited at the International Exhibition, Vienna, in 1892. It was reproduced in facsimile in *Chopin (Life and Work)*, vol. 1, by Ferdinand Hoesick, Warsaw, 1910. For its republication as the third of 'Three Polonaises', see 1.

MS. Society of Music, Warsaw.

6

POLONAISE in G sharp minor. 1822

Publication:

> Josef Kauffmann, Warsaw (. . .). 1864.
> B. Schott's Sons, Mainz (17,943). 1864.

Dedicated to Mme. (Sofie?) Dupont. The Duponts were

French friends of the composer's family. The marriage of one of Mme. Dupont's daughters is mentioned by Chopin in his letter of 15 May 1830.

Niecks was of the opinion that the 'internal evidence of the work' pointed to a later date than 1822: the Gebethner edition (1878) is dated '1824'.

Kauffmann published the work in a series called 'Compositions modernes et classiques pour piano'. There were thirty-two pieces in the series, Chopin's 'Polonez' being 'No. 32'. No Publisher's Number is printed on the publication.

MS. Lost.

7

MAZURKA in A flat major, Op. 7: no. 4 (first version). 1824

Publication:

A facsimile reproduction is given in *Chopin in der Heimat*, Cracow, 1955, page 84.

The Mazurka was written for the composer's school-friend Wilhelm Kolberg (1809–1877).

The manuscript bears, in the hand of Oscar Kolberg, Wilhelm's brother, the words: 'Written by Fr. Chopin in the year 1824'. The section in D flat major is entitled by the composer on this manuscript 'Trio'.

For the final version, see **61**.

MS. Society of Music, Warsaw.

8

MAZURKA in A minor, Op. 17: no. 4 (first version). August 1824

This may be the work referred to by Chopin in the little mock newspaper (3 September 1824 'issue') which he and his sister Emilia devised for family reading and amusement in the summer of 1824 from Szafarnia (the 'Szafarnian Courier'). He reported '. . . Mr. Pichon [an anagram of Chopin] played "The Little Jew".' The tentative suggestion was first put forward by Marcel Antoine Szulc (1873); it has been taken up by subsequent biographers as if it were an established fact.

Szafarnia was part of the estate of the friend of the Chopin family, Dominik Dzyewanowski.

For the final version, see 77.

MS. Lost.

9

VARIATIONS in E major for Flute and Pianoforte on a theme from Rossini's *La Cenerentola*. (?) 1824

Publication:

A facsimile reproduction in *Chopin in der Heimat*, Cracow, 1955, page 269.

The theme is no. 12 of the opera, the Finale, 'Della fortuna istabile' (also in E major). The Variations are said to have been written by Chopin for Josef Cichocki, a famous flute-player in Warsaw. The manuscript was formerly in the possession of Josef Nowakowski.

MS. Society of Music, Warsaw.

RONDO in C minor, Op. 1. May 1825

Publication:

> Andrea Brzezina, Warsaw. June 1825.
> Republished by:
>
> > (*a*) A. M. Schlesinger, Berlin (2019). December 1835.
> > (*b*) M. Schlesinger, Paris (1986). January 1836.
> > (*c*) Wessel, London (1423). March 1836.
> > (*d*) Hofmeister, Leipzig (2375). 1838.

Dedicated to Mme. Linde, wife of Dr. Samuel Bogmul Linde, philologist, friend and colleague of Nicolas Chopin, and Rector of the Warsaw Conservatoire.

It was announced in the Warsaw *Kuryer*, 2 June 1825, by Brzezina, and published by him without opus number (also without Publisher's Number). It was called 'Opus 1' on republication in Berlin. Brzezina's firm was taken over by Gustav Sennewald, Warsaw, *c.* 1830. On 27 November 1831 Louise Chopin wrote to her brother: 'Hofmeister has written to Sennewald to send him all your works, those already printed and those to be printed.'

Wessel entitled his edition *Adieu à Varsovie*. It formed no. 1 of his series 'L'amateur Pianiste'.

The work has been erroneously called 'Rondeau on *Don Giovanni*', through confusion with the composer's Op. 2.

MS. Lost.

Lost work of 1825:

> In November 1825 Chopin wrote to Białobłocki: 'I

have done a new Polonaise on the "Barber" [Rossini's *Barber of Seville*] which is fairly well liked; I think of sending it to be lithographed tomorrow.' (For Białobłocki, see 1).

II

POLONAISE in D minor, Op. 71: no. 1 (Posth.). 1825

Publication:

    A. M. Schlesinger, Berlin (4397). May 1855.
    J. Meissonnier fils, Paris (3528). February 1856.

Composed for Count Michel Skarbek. Chopin sent a copy of the Polonaise to Titus Woyciechowski in 1827, but the work was not dedicated to him.

Meissonnier's editions of the posthumous works were published without opus numbers. They were simply called *Livraisons I–VII.*

A facsimile of a fragmentary manuscript of the work was given in the *Illustrowany Kuryer Codzienny,* Cracow, 24 September 1934. (See 17).

MS. Arthur Hedley, London. There are no tempo or expression marks on the manuscript. The date is as estimated by Mr. Hedley, who is of the opinion that the MS. may be in the hand of the composer's father, Nicolas Chopin.

THREE ÉCOSSAISES, Op. 72: no. 3 (Posth.). 1826

>No. 1 in D major.
>No. 2 in G major.
>No. 3 in D flat major.

For publication of Op. 72, see **19**.

Several écossaises were composed at this period; only these have survived. See note after **17**.

MSS. Nos. 2 and 3, written on page 2 of the song 'Piosńka Litewska' ('Lithuanian Song'): Memorial Library of Music, Stanford University, California.

Lost works of 1826:

>(*a*) Variations in F major for PF. Duet.
>(*b*) Variations on an Irish National Air (from Thomas Moore) for PF. Duet.
>(*c*) Waltz in C major.

All three works are listed by Louise Chopin, but the manuscripts were evidently lost before they could be published.

The Variations in F major were composed for Titus Woyciechowski (1810–1889), the most intimate of Chopin's friends, a friendship dating from boyhood. Woyciechowski's estate was at Poturżyn.

The Irish Variations are stated to be in 'D major or B minor' and the time-signature is given as 6/8.

13

POLONAISE in B flat minor. July 1826

Publication:

> The Polonaise had been lithographed for Chopin in Warsaw in 1826. It was republished as a supplement to the *Echo Muzyczne*, Warsaw, no. 12, 3 June 1881.
>
> Breitkopf & Haertel, Leipzig: *Gesamtausgabe* of Chopin's works, vol. XIII, no. 16 (C.XIII.2). December 1879.

The work was composed for Wilhelm Kolberg (7) on the occasion of Chopin's departure with his sister Emilia for the spa Reinertz. He and Kolberg had recently visited the National Theatre, Warsaw, to see Rossini's *La Gazza Ladra*. Chopin has headed his original sketch: 'Polonaise. F. F. Chopin' and above the Trio he has written 'Au revoir!'. Another hand (probably Kolberg's or his brother's) has added to the title: 'Adieu à Guil. Kolberg (en partant pour Reinertz) 1826.', and to the Trio: 'Trio tiré d'un air de la Gazza Ladra par Rossini.' At the foot of the Trio these words, partly cancelled, have been added by the same hand: 'Quelques jours avant son depart, Ch. accompagné de Kolberg [. . . .?] une represtation de la Gazza Ladra de Rossini.'

The air, a short Cavatina, was a favourite of Kolberg's. It is 'Vieni fra questa braccia' ('Come to these arms'), Act. I, no. 6, and is sung by Gianetto (tenor) to the maid Ninetta.

Rossini's aria is *maestoso*, in D major.[1] *La Gazza Ladra* was first performed at La Scala, Milan, 31 May 1817.

MS. Original draft: Paris Conservatoire. This manuscript contains a substantial sketch for a 'Mazur Oberski' in C major.

14

INTRODUCTION AND VARIATIONS in E major, on a German National Air ['Der Schweizerbub']. Summer 1826

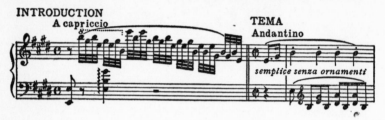

Publication:

> Karl (Tobias) Haslinger, Vienna (T.H. 8148). May 1851.
> Simon Richault, Paris (10869). May 1851.
> Cocks, London (9728). January 1852.

Dedicated to Katarina Sowińska, *née* Schroeder, wife of General Josef Sowiński. Chopin is said to have written these variations for Mme. Sowińska at her request, after she had heard the air sung by Henrietta Sontag, but she could not, in fact, have heard the singer until 1830, at the earliest. Louise mentioned her in the letter to Chopin of 27 November 1831: 'Mme Sowińska always enquires after you with the greatest affection.'

The folk-song is Austrian, probably Tyrolean (see *Deutscher Liederhort*, L. Erk and F. M. Boehme, vol. III). Moscheles is said to have taken down and arranged the traditional airs of a group of Tyrolean singers who visited London in 1827: one of these airs was 'Der Schweizerbub'. Particulars are given in *Grove's Dictionary*, vol. III under 'Moscheles'. The first verse runs:

[1] See *Musical Times*, London, August 1954.

Steh nur auf, steh nur auf du junger Schweizerbua,
Steh nur auf, es ist jetzt Zeit!
Steh nur in Gottes Namen auf.
Deine Kuha die sind schon auf der Alma drauf.
Steh nur auf, du junger Schweizerbua!

The title means 'the cattleboy' and would seem to be mistranslated if rendered as 'the Swiss boy'.

The Introduction is *a capriccio*, there are five variations. Chopin's direction *semplice senza ornamenti* reveals the contemporary habit of embellishment in performance.

Chopin deposited the manuscript with Tobias Haslinger in Vienna during his first visit to the city in August 1829. The Publisher's Number shows that publication was contemplated in 1840 (see also **23**).

Cocks's edition was no. 14 of a series called 'The Classical Pianist: a Selection of Movements from the Works of the Great Masters', edited by Brinley Richards.

MS. Library of the Polish Academy of Science, Cracow. It is inscribed by Oscar Kolberg: 'I received the manuscript from the wife of General Sowiński in 1852, and presented it to the Cracow Library on 19 June 1874.' This copy is not an autograph of Chopin's.

15

RONDO à la Mazur, in F major, Op. 5. 1826

Publication:

Andrea Brzezina, Warsaw. 28 February 1828.
Republished by:

(*a*) Hofmeister, Leipzig (2121). May 1836.
(*b*) Schonenberger, Paris (608). May 1836.
(*c*) Wessel, London (1552). October 1837.

Dedicated to Mlle. la Comtesse Alexandrina de Moriolles, daughter of Count de Moriolles and a pupil of Chopin. Her father was tutor to the son of the Grand Duke Constantine.

The work was published without opus number by Brzezina. It was called 'Op. 5' by Hofmeister, and Chopin had obviously reserved this number for the Rondo: by 1836 his other opus numbers had reached 27.

For Brzezina and Hofmeister, see 10.

Wessel's edition, also without opus number, was called *Rondo à la Majourka*; later this was changed to *La Posiana: Rondo on a Mazur in F*. Wessel claimed that it was 'Edited by his pupil I. [*sic*] Fontana'. He re-issued the Rondo *c*. 1846 as no. 11 of the series called 'Le Pianiste Moderne', advertised as a continuation of the series 'L'amateur Pianiste'. His Publisher's Number suggests that publication was delayed.

MS. Lost.

16

TWO MAZURKAS. 1826

No. 1 in G major.
No. 2 in B flat major.

Each Mazurka exists in two versions.

Publication:

First versions.

M. Leitgeber, Poznań, as no. 2 and no. 3 of three mazurkas (M.L. 18). 5 January 1875.

Republished by Breitkopf & Haertel, Leipzig, in the Chopin *Gesamtausgabe*, vol. XIII. 17 December 1879.

Second versions.

Warsaw, 1826. Each in a small, oblong format, without title or publisher's name.

Republished by R. Friedlein, Warsaw (R. 25 F.). May 1851.

The history of the publication of the two versions of these two mazurkas is complex and obscure. The above facts present the most likely explanation. Both versions of each mazurka are published in the 'Mazurkas' volume of the Polish 'Complete Edition' (vol. X), but the account given (in the appendix of the volume) of the publication of them is unsatisfactory, principally because the date of Friedlein's publication seems not to be known, and also because various reprints of the above editions in the Warsaw *Echo Muzyczne* and elsewhere seem to be treated as original sources.

Both mazurkas, together with the one in D major (below), were said to be improvised by Chopin during dancing entertainments at the home of Dr. Samuel Linde, the Rector of the Warsaw Conservatoire (*c.* 1826) and written down by friends of the composer. The Mazurka in G major was known to them as the 'Kulawy' Mazurka due to the style of the dance ('Kulawy'=lame).

Chopin left the first versions of the two mazurkas, in manuscript, with his friend Wilhelm Kolberg, from whose brother, Oscar, resident in Cracow, they passed eventually to M. A. Szulc, who edited them for Leitgeber. The composer's second versions were lithographed in Warsaw, with his permission, in 1826 and he is supposed to have revised a copy of this printing in his own hand. This revised copy was

Friedlein's source; it went into the possession of Alexander Poliński (see 3) but is no longer extant.

Leitgeber's publication, with a foreword by M. A. Szulc, also included the Mazurka in D major (31) as no. 1 and the 'Lento con gran espressione' (49). Brahms, on his copy of this publication, wrote the words: 'Vol. XIII, no. 1, comp. 1825' and 'Vol. XIII, no. 2, comp. 1825' above the mazurkas respectively. This indicated their future positions in the Breitkopf & Haertel *Gesamtausgabe*.

The first Mazurka, in G major, may have been performed by Chopin in August 1826, while he was at Reinertz.

In his letter to Jan Białobłocki of 8 January 1827, Chopin wrote of these two mazurkas: 'They are already published; meanwhile I am leaving my Rondo à la Mazur, that I wanted to have lithographed, stifling among my papers, though it is earlier and therefore has more right to travel.'

MSS. Lost.

17

CONTREDANSE in G flat major. (?) 1827

Publication:

    A facsimile reproduction in the *Illustrowany Kuryer Codzienny* ('Illustrated Daily Courier'): Literary and Scientific Supplement, Cracow, 24 September 1934.

The Dance, twenty-seven bars long, was composed for Titus Woyciechowski (see note after 12). The further information, that it was written for his 'name-day' (4 January) or for his birthday (4 March) 1829, arises from the fact that, associated with the manuscript, another music page was found; it bore those dates and Chopin's signature. But the pieces of music paper are quite unalike, and since the dates and signature are written below the heading: 'Introduction & Variations pour le pianoforte', the second paper evidently belongs to Op. 2 (**22**) and not to the Contredanse at all.

The facsimile was reproduced also in *Szlakiem Chopina* by Maria Mirska, Warsaw, 1935. The Dance, edited by Michael Idzikowski, was printed in Warsaw in 1943.

MS. This was preserved by the descendants of Woyciechowski, but destroyed in the Second World War.

Lost works of 1827:
- (*a*) Écossaise in B flat major.
- (*b*) *Andante dolente* in B flat minor.

Both works are mentioned in the list of unpublished works compiled by Louise Chopin, the composer's sister. *Dolente*= doleful.

18

MAZURKA in A minor, Op. 68: no. 2 (Posth.). 1827

Publication of Op. 68:
> A. M. Schlesinger, Berlin (4394). May 1855.
> J. Meissonnier fils, Paris (3525). February 1856.

Meissonnier's editions of the posthumous works were published without opus numbers.

MS. Lost.

NOCTURNE in E minor, Op. 72: no. 1 (Posth.). 1827

Publication of Op. 72:

    A. M. Schlesinger, Berlin (4400). May 1855.

    J. Meissonnier fils, Paris (3531). February 1856.

Meissonnier's editions of the posthumous works were published without opus numbers.

MS. Lost.

20

FUNERAL MARCH in C minor, Op. 72: no. 2 (Posth.). 1827

Publication:

    Version (*a*): A. M. Schlesinger, Berlin (4400). May 1855.

             J. Meissonnier fils, Paris (3531). February 1856.

    Version (*b*): Oxford Edition of *Chopin's Works*, vol. III: edited by E. Ganche. London, 1932.

The date is according to Louise's list; Fontana gives 1829. Meissonnier's editions of the posthumous works were published without opus numbers.

MSS. 1. Version (*a*): Lost.
     2. Version (*b*): A copy of this version, made by Tellefsen in May 1850 for Marcellina Czartoryska, with Arthur Hedley, London.

21

WALTZ in A flat major. 1827

Publication:
    Breitkopf & Haertel, Leipzig, in a supplement to the *Gesamtausgabe* of Chopin's works ('Klavierbibliothek', 23, 183 : II). 1902.
    F. Hoesick, Warsaw. 1902.

The Waltz was discovered in an album which had belonged to Emily Elsner, the daughter of Josef Elsner (see **23**). Her album also contained a Waltz in E flat (**46**), the first version of the Mazurka in A minor, Op. 7: no. 2 (**45**) and seven of the songs of Op. 74 (see Appendix VIII for details). Breitkopf & Haertel, in their supplement, published the three instrumental pieces.

There was another copy of this Waltz originally among the Chopin family papers.

MSS. (1) Lost.
    (2) Emily Elsner's Album: (destroyed) formerly with the Society of Music, Warsaw.

22

VARIATIONS in B flat major on a theme from Mozart's *Don Giovanni* (Là ci darem la mano'), for PF. and Orchestra, Op. 2. Strzyżewo, late summer 1827

Publication:

> Tobias Haslinger, Vienna (5489). January 1830.
> M. Schlesinger, Paris (1312). Early 1833.
> Wessel, London (820). Spring 1833.

Dedicated to Titus Woyciechowski (see note after **12** and **17**).

The theme comes from the duet sung by Don Giovanni and Zerlina in Act I, no. 7. Schumann's article containing the words 'Hats off, gentlemen, a genius!' deals with this work of Chopin's.

Strzyżewo is a country place some 150 miles to the south-west of Warsaw.

The work was first performed by the composer on 11 August 1829 in the Kärntnertor Theater, Vienna. The performance in Warsaw followed on 8 July 1830 at a concert given by the singer Mme. Meyer.

The Variations were published as 'Lieferung 27' in Haslinger's serial publication *Odéon*, described as 'Ausgewählte grosse Concert-Stücke für verschiedene Instrumente' ('Selected Grand Concert Pieces for various instruments'); it was the first of Chopin's compositions to be published outside Poland. The manuscript was in Haslinger's hands by the summer of 1828, sent to him by Josef Elsner (see next). In 1839 Haslinger published an arrangement for PF. Solo (T.H. 7714).

Wessel's edition is entitled *Homage* [*sic*] *à Mozart* and forms Book XVII of the 'Album des Pianistes de Première Force'; this is described as 'A Collection of the most Brilliant and Original Compositions' and contained pieces by Hummel, Czerny, Pixis among others. The English edition was dedicated without authorisation to Charles Czerny.

The French edition was based on a printed copy of the Viennese edition corrected by Chopin himself.

The manuscript in the Vienna Nationalbibliothek (see below) contains a cancelled variation, the fourth, and in its place Chopin has brought forward the original no. 6.[1] The work thus contained in its first form *seven* variations, the last serving as a finale. The cancelled variation is reproduced in Franz Zagiba's *Chopin und Wien*, Vienna, 1951, page 24.

MSS. (1) Nationalbibliothek, Vienna.
     (2) Two pages containing the beginning of Variation V (*adagio*): Maison Pleyel

Lost work of 1828:
    Waltz in D minor.
The work is given in Louise's list, with the date, and entitled (? by Louise) 'La Partenza' ('The Departure').

[1] See *Musical Times*, London, August 1954.

SONATA in C minor, Op. 4 (Posth.). Early 1828

Publication:

> Karl Haslinger, Vienna (T.H. 8147). May 1851.
> Simon Richault, Paris (10868). May 1851.
> Cocks, London (9727). January 1852.

Dedicated to Josef Elsner (1769–1854), Silesian composer and first principal of the Warsaw Conservatoire, Chopin's tutor in composition. It was he who sent the MS. of the Sonata to Haslinger in the summer of 1828. Chopin wrote: 'As a pupil of Elsner's I dedicated [the Sonata] to him.' Elsner's acceptance of the dedication is written on the autograph in his own hand. The inscription on the MS. reads:

> Sonata pour le pianoforte dediée à Mr. Josef Elsner, Professeur à l'Université Royale de Varsovie, Membre de la Société Philomatique de Varsovie, Chevalier de l'ordre de St. Stanislas, etc., etc. Composée par Frédéric Chopin. Oeuvre 3 [*sic*].

The real Op. 3 (41) had appeared in 1831–1833, and so the opus number of the Sonata was altered to 4. Karl Haslinger published the work without the dedication to Elsner. His father and predecessor in the business, Tobias Haslinger, had engraved the Sonata as early as the summer of 1839, which accounts for the 'Publisher's Number'. Chopin refused to correct the proofs. But Haslinger must have passed the proofs privately to musicians in Germany and Austria, for during August 1839 Chopin wrote to Julian Fontana: 'My father writes that my old Sonata has been published by Haslinger and that the Germans praise it.' Several years later he wrote to his family on 1 October 1845: 'The Sonata dedicated to Elsner has been published in Vienna by Haslinger.'

The London publication was referred to by Jane Stirling in her letter to Louise Chopin of January 1852. It is no. 13 of a series called 'The Classical Pianist' (see 14).

MS. Louis Koch Collection: Rudolf Floersheim, Muzzano-Lugano, Switzerland, dated '1828'.

24

POLONAISE in B flat major, Op. 71: no. 2 (Posth.). 1828

Publication:

> A. M. Schlesinger, Berlin (4398). May 1855.
> J. Meissonnier fils, Paris (3529). February 1856.

Meissonnier's editions of the posthumous works were published without opus numbers.

MS. Arthur Hedley, London (there are no tempo or expression marks of any kind). It contains the first few bars of the Polonaise in F minor (30).

TRIO in G minor, for PF., vn. and cello, Op. 8. Poznań, mid-1828—Warsaw, early 1829

Publication:

> H. A. Probst-F. Kistner, Leipzig (999). December 1832.
> M. Schlesinger, Paris (1344). November 1833.
> Wessel, London (924). July 1833.

Dedicated to Prince Antoine Radziwill (1775–1833), German-Polish cellist and composer, Governor of the Grand Duchy of Poznań. He accepted the dedication in a warm letter of thanks to Chopin dated 4 November 1829.

The work was published in Leipzig as *Premier Trio*. The first movement, 'Allegro', was finished by early September

1828 and the composer in a letter of 27 December 1828 to Titus Woyciechowski referred to the whole work as 'not quite finished'. In a letter to the same friend of 31 August 1830, Chopin wondered whether to rewrite the work with viola instead of violin.

Schlesinger's edition was a republication in Paris of what had hitherto been an exclusive German publication. At that date he also brought out the mazurkas, Opp. 6 and 7 (**60 and 61**), which had previously been published only by Probst-Kistner in Leipzig.

Op. 8 was often missing from Wessel's advertised lists of the English edition of the composer's works. He published an arrangement of the work by T. Clinton for Flute, cello and PF. (Publisher's Number 930). In September 1838 he issued it as no. 1 of a series of 'Modern Trios for PF., vn. & cello'.

Occasionally Wessel (e.g. in 1841) advertised the first two Nocturnes of Op. 9 as 'Op. 8', calling the third Nocturne 'Op. 9'.

MSS. (1) Sketches for the Trio, including others for the PF. Concerto, Op. 21:

(2) Fair copy of the score:

Both MSS. in the Chopin Institute, Warsaw.

26

RONDO in C major, for PF. Solo, Op. 73 (original version). Sanniki, summer 1828

Publication:

Vol. XII of the *Dzieła Wszystkie* ('Complete Works') of Chopin, Warsaw. 1954.

A facsimile of part of the autograph was reproduced in *Chopin und Wien*, Franz Zagiba, Vienna, 1951, page 112. A facsimile of the whole autograph (four pages) is given in the Warsaw edition.

The autograph manuscript contains in Chopin's hand: 'à M. Fuchs. F. F. Chopin', and in Fuchs's hand: 'Received from the composer himself, as a gift, and bequeathed to the Musikverein here by Alois Fuchs, Vienna, November 1840.' Chopin gave Fuchs the manuscript in June 1831.

Sanniki is a small country district some fifty miles south-west of Warsaw. It belonged to a family named Pruszak, friends of the composer.

MS. Gesellschaft der Musikfreunde, Vienna (the Musik-verein).

27

RONDO in C major, for Two Pianofortes, Op. 73 (final version) (Posth.). Sanniki, August 1828

Publication:

    A. M. Schlesinger, Berlin (4401). May 1855.

    J. Meissonnier fils, Paris (3532). February 1856.

Meissonnier's editions of the posthumous works were published without opus numbers. Schlesinger also published arrangements for PF. Duet (Op. 73 A) and for PF. Solo (Op. 73 B).

The work is an arrangement of the previous item by Chopin. In a letter to Woyciechowski of 9 September 1828 he wrote: 'Today I tried it with Ernemann at Buchholtz's [a PF. manufacturer] and it came out pretty well. We think of playing it some day at the Ressource.' Later, on 27 December 1828, in another letter to the same friend, he referred to it as 'that orphan child' which had found a stepfather in Julian Fontana (see 120).

The Ressource was a private association of musical amateurs in Warsaw. For Sanniki, see previous item.

MS. Lost.

28

GRAND FANTASIA in A major, on Polish Airs, for PF. and Orchestra, Op. 13. November 1828

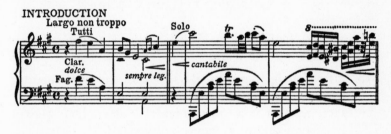

Publication:
    Probst-Kistner, Leipzig (1033–1034). May 1834.
    M. Schlesinger, Paris (1574). April 1834.
    Wessel, London (1083). May 1834.

(This is the first work of Chopin's to be published simultaneously in Germany, France and England. The practice persisted for the next thirteen years until the publication of Op. 64.)

Dedicated to Johann Peter Pixis (1788–1874), German pianist and composer, resident in Paris from 1825 to 1845.

Among the Polish airs used are these:

(*a*) The folk-song 'Już miesiąc zaszedł, psy się uspiły' ('Already the moon had set, the dogs were asleep');
(*b*) an air by Karol (Kasimir) Kurpiński;
(*c*) a *Kujawiak*, which is a dance of the Kujawia district,

called by Chopin a 'Mazovian air'. ('The *Kujawiak* is a species of Mazurka—according to all the authorities the slowest kind of Mazurka, though Chopin marks his *vivace*.' Gerald Abraham, *Chopin's musical style*, London, 1939, page 23.)

Kistner issued the Fantasia in two versions, with and without orchestral accompaniment.

Wessel published the work as Book XXI of the 'Album des Pianistes de Première Force' (see **22**) and claimed that it, as well as Opp. 14, 21 and 22, were expressly composed for the series.

The first performance of the Fantasia took place on 3 March 1830 in the National Theatre, Warsaw, with the composer as soloist.

Kurpiński (1785–1857), Polish violinist and composer, was a professor at the Warsaw Conservatoire.

MS.   First sketch, fragment. Bars 1–20 of the Introduction, bars 34 and 35 (PF. part only) of the Fantasia, with sketches for the instrumental parts: Dr. Martin Bodmer, Coligny, Geneva, Switzerland.

29

KRAKOWIAK: Grand Concert Rondo in F major, for PF. and Orchestra, Op. 14. November to December 1828

Publication:

Probst-Kistner, Leipzig (1038–1039). July 1834.

M. Schlesinger, Paris (1586). June 1834.
Wessel, London (1084). May 1834.

Dedicated to Mme. la Princesse Adam Czartoryska (Marcellina, *née* Radziwill), exiled Polish Princess, pupil and lifelong friend of Chopin.

In a letter of 27 December 1828 to Woyciechowski, the composer wrote: 'The score of the *Rondo à la Krakowiak* is finished.'

A *Krakowiak* is a Polish dance in 2/4 time of the Cracow district.

Probst-Kistner issued the work with and without orchestral accompaniment. This was Chopin's last publication in Leipzig from Probst-Kistner; after this his work was published by Breitkopf & Haertel.

Wessel published the work as XXII of his 'Album des Pianistes de Première Force' (see 22 and previous item.)

Schlesinger simultaneously published arrangements of the orchestral part for (*a*) string quartet and (*b*) a second piano.

MS. Czartoryski Library, National Museum, Cracow. The manuscript is now bound in green plush, with the Bovy medallion-portrait of Chopin stamped on the cover in gilt. It was presented by Chopin, with an autograph dedication, to his friend Adolf Cichowski (1794–1854). The composer added: 'published in 1831 or 1832', which is, of course, an imperfect memory.

30

POLONAISE in F minor, Op. 71: no. 3 (Posth.). 1828

Publication:

A. M. Schlesinger, Berlin (4399). May 1855.

J. Meissonnier fils, Paris (3530). February 1856.

Meissonnier's editions of the posthumous works were published without opus numbers.

The date is according to Louise's list; Fontana gives 1829.

The work was played and greatly liked by Princess Radziwill during Chopin's visit to Antonin in October 1829.

MSS. (1) Sketch of the first few bars, dated 1829 (see **24**): Arthur Hedley, London.

(2) Fair copy, dated 'Stuttgart, 1836': unknown.

31

MAZURKA in D major (first version). 1829

Publication:

M. Leitgeber, Poznań (M.L. 18). 5 January 1875.

Leitgeber's edition, edited and with a foreword by M. A. Szulc, included the Mazurkas in G major and B flat major (**16**) and the 'Lento con gran espressione' (**49**).

The work was revised considerably in 1832 (see **72**).

Brahms wrote on his copy: 'Bd. XIII: no. 6. comp. 1829.' This indicated its future position in the Breitkopf & Haertel *Gesamtausgabe* (see **16**).

MS. Lost.

32

SONG for voice and PF., Op. 74: no. 5. 1829

'Gdzie lubi' ('Strumyk lubi w dolinie')

'There where she loves' ('A stream loves the vale').
(A major)

German title: 'Was ein junges Mädchen liebt.'
Text: Stefan Witwicki.

Publication of Op. 74:

A. M. Schlesinger, Berlin
(*a*) A Polish edition entitled: *Zbior Śpiewow Polskich*
('A Collection of Polish Songs') (4638–4653). 1857.
(*b*) A German edition, with translations by Ferdinand
Gumbert [no Polish text interlined] (4797–4812).
Op. 74: nos. 1–4, December 1859; Op. 74: nos.
5–16, January 1860.

Gebethner, Warsaw (84–99). 1859.

Op. 74 contained originally only sixteen songs. No. 17,
'Śpiew Grobowy' ('Hymn from the Tomb'), was added
later, *c*. 1868 (see **101**).

The complete seventeen songs of Op. 74 were issued later
by:

(*a*) A. M. Schlesinger, Berlin, in two versions: for
Soprano or Tenor (6669) and for Alto or Bass (6670).
1874.
(*b*) Karl Haslinger, Vienna, *c*. 1870.
(*c*) Breitkopf & Haertel, Leipzig, with new translations
by Hans Schmidt, *c*. 1874.
(*d*) Stanley Lucas, Weber & Co., London (299), with
English translations by the Rev. J. J. Troutbeck, from
the German text by Gumbert, 1874.
(*e*) J. Hamelle, Paris (1467), June 1879.
(*f*) Gebethner & Wolff, Warsaw, 1880.

Peters' Edition of the songs, *c.* 1887, with translations by Wilhelm Henzen and Max Kalbeck, still contained only the original sixteen songs.

Two of the songs from Op. 74—no. 10, 'Wojak' ('The Warrior') and no. 1, 'Życzenie' ('The Wish') (see **47** and **33**)—had already been published as 2 *Śpiéwy* ('2 Songs') by A. Kocipiński, Kiev (44 and 48) in 1856. These were probably re-issues of an anonymous publication by the same firm in 1837.[1]

Gebethner used Schlesinger's plates for the edition of 1859, which was reviewed by Josef Sowiński in the *Revue Musicale*, Warsaw, no. 40, 1859.

Wessel had refused the songs in 1854 as unsaleable in England, although he was referring to a *Polish text* edition.

The songs of Op. 74, together with two further songs not included there (**51** and **132**), are published in the Polish 'Complete Edition', Vol. XVII, 1951.

In the announcement of a concert given in Paris on 14 January 1856, Fontana referred to the six Polish songs in the programme as still unpublished. This disposes of the date usually given (1855) for the publication of Op. 74. Fontana contributed a foreword to Schlesinger's editions of the songs.

The poems by Witwicki which Chopin set to music were all published in his *Piośnki Sielski* ('Pastoral Songs'), Warsaw, 1830. The composer, however, knew them in manuscript (see **51**).

MSS. (1) Emily Elsner's Album (now destroyed).
(2) Maria Wodzińska's Album: State Collection, Warsaw.

There is a complete manuscript transcript of the songs, used by Schlesinger for the 1859 publication, and made by Fontana and another (? Franchomme) in the possession of Antony van Hoboken, Ascona, Switzerland.

[1] See the *Musical Quarterly*, New York, January 1956.

33

SONG for voice and PF., Op. 74: no. 1. 1829

'Życzenie' ('Gdy bym była słoneczkiem na ')
'The Wish' ('Were I the sun in the sky')

(G major)

German title: 'Mädchens Wunsch'.
Text: Stefan Witwicki.

Publication:

    Anton Kocipiński, Kiev (48). *c.* 1856. This was probably
a republication of an anonymous edition of the song by
this firm from 1837.

For details of its publication in Op. 74, see **32**.

    Fontana transposed the song into A major for the Op. 74
edition, and made several alterations in the musical text.
Chopin's version of the opening is given here under (*a*),
Fontana's alteration under (*b*).

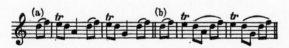

    Liszt used the song as no. 2 of his *Glanes de Woronince*,
calling it 'Melodie Polonaise'. He was under the impression
that it was a folk-song, and thus he may have used the
Kocipiński copy of the 1837 edition mentioned above.
Glanes de Woronince was published by Kistner of Leipzig in
1849.

Liszt also transcribed the song for PF. Solo (6 *Chants Polonais:* no. 1), published by A. M. Schlesinger, 1860.

'Życzenie' was transposed into B flat major and furnished with words by George Sand. Her poem begins:

> Quand la lune se leve / Dans un pale rayon,
> Elle vient comme un reve, / Comme un vision.

This version was published as 'La Reine des Songes' in the *Journal de Musique*, Paris, no. 8, 22 July 1876. The *Journal* published several music supplements by Chopin in 1876–1877; the July issue was devoted to George Sand and Chopin. It contained as supplements these three pieces:

(*a*) 'La Reine des Songes',
(*b*) *Rondo* (extracted from Op. 11),
(*c*) 74 bars in A minor, from the 'Bolero', Op. 19, entitled 'Chanson de Zingara: souvenir du voyage en Espagne' (see **81**).

There were three autographs of this song. (1) A copy in the possession of the Chopin family was first reproduced in 1901 by Michael Karlowicz in his book now generally known in its French version: *Souvenirs inédits de Chopin*, Paris, 1904. (2) A copy in Emily Elsner's Album. (3) A copy in Maria Wodzinska's Album (1836). Particulars are given below.

MSS. (1) Leopold Binental's Collection: lost in the Second World War.

(2) Society of Music, Warsaw: destroyed in the Second World War.

(3) State Collection, Warsaw.

34

MAZURKA in F major, Op. 68: no. 3 (Posth.). 1829

Publication of Op. 68:

    A. M. Schlesinger, Berlin (4394). May 1855.

    J. Meissonnier fils, Paris (3525). February 1856.

Meissonnier's editions of the posthumous works were published without opus numbers.

The section *poco più vivo* is from the folk-tune 'Oj Magdalino':

MS. Lost.

35

WALTZ in B minor, Op. 69: no. 2 (Posth.). 1829

Publication:

    J. Wildt, Cracow (No Publisher's Number). 1852.

    Wessel, London (8015). July 1853.

    Republished as Op. 69: no. 2 by:

    A. M. Schlesinger, Berlin (4395). May 1855.

    J. Meissonnier fils, Paris (3526). February 1856.

Meissonnier's editions of the posthumous works were published without opus numbers.

Wildt's publication, which also included the Waltz in F minor, Op. 70: no. 2 (**138**), was entitled:

> Une soirée en 1844. Deux valses mélancholiques
> écrites sur l'album de Mme. la Comtesse Pxxx.

The Countess was probably Delphine Potocka (**43**), but the waltz in B minor was originally written for Wilhelm Kolberg (see **7**).

Wessel's title was similar to that of the original publisher but with the characteristic addition: 'Une soirée à Cracovie en 1844. . . .'

The two waltzes were also published in England (April 1854) by J. J. Ewer, London.

Fontana was aware of the fact that the two waltzes were already published when he included them in the posthumous opus numbers which he sponsored in 1855. This is clear from the letter which he received from Breitkopf & Haertel on 14 March 1854. His manuscript is lost.

MSS. (1) The copy in Delphine Potocka's Album: unknown. It was formerly in the possession of Alexander Tyszkiewicz, Mohylow.

(2) Bibliothek Jagielloński, Cracow University. This MS. is inscribed by Oscar Kolberg, the brother of Wilhelm, who presented it to Cracow University on 29 March 1881. This was used as the basis of the waltz published in Vol. I of the *Oxford Edition of Chopin's Works*, London, 1932.

36

POLONAISE in G flat major. 1829 (probably before July, when Chopin left Warsaw for Vienna)

Publication:

  J. Kauffmann, Warsaw (170). 1870.

  B. Schott's Sons, Mainz (20,029). 1870.

  Republished by:

  (*a*) *Die Musik*, Berlin. October 1908;

  (*b*) Leon Chojecki, Warsaw. 1909.

  Both these republications were erroneously believed to be first editions.

The Polonaise, fifty-eight bars long, with a Trio in E flat minor of seventy bars, is named in Louise's list, so that the MS. was extant in the 1850's. Niecks queried the authenticity of the work: 'Nothing but the composer's autograph would convince one of the genuineness of the piece.'

MS. Lost.

37

VARIATIONS in A major ('Souvenir de Paganini'). Summer 1829

Publication:

  Supplement to *Echo Muzyczne*, Warsaw, no. 5, 1881

The work is quite short, ninety-one bars. The manuscript was formerly in the possession of Chopin's friend, Josef Nowakowski, and from him it passed to the Warsaw composer and music teacher Adam Minhejmer,[1] who secured its publication. Jan Kleczyński wrote a preface for this publication. The work was republished in vol. XIII of the Polish 'Complete Edition', 1954.

---

[1] Better known by the German form of his name, Münchheimer. In 1892 he also owned the MSS. of **5**, **9** and **28**.

The theme of these variations is the Italian air 'Le Carnival de Venise' used by Paganini himself as the basis of variations in his Op. 10. Ludwig Bronarski suggested that Paganini may have played this Op. 10 during his visit to Warsaw (23 May to 19 July 1829), and that Chopin heard his playing of it.

MS. Unknown. It was exhibited at the International Exhibition, Vienna, 1892.

38

MAZURKA in C major, Op. 68: no. 1 (Posth.). 1829

Publication of Op. 68:

    A. M. Schlesinger, Berlin (4394). May 1855.

    J. Meissonnier fils, Paris (3525). February 1856.

Meissonnier's editions of the posthumous works were published without opus numbers.

MS. Lost.

39

MAZURKA in G major. 22 August 1829

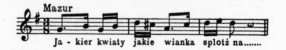

Publication:

    Dalibor, Prague, no. 6, 20 February 1879.

The piece was written in the Album of Vaclav Hanka

(1791–1861), philologist and librarian, the curator of the Prague Museum. Chopin wrote to his family from Dresden on 26 August 1829: 'Luckily Macicowski hit on the idea of writing a four-verse Mazurka, so I set it to music and inscribed myself together with my poet as originally as possible.'

Ignac Macicowski accompanied the composer on the return journey from Vienna to Warsaw. His poem celebrates Czech-Polish friendship and actually consists of five, not four, verses. It begins:

> Jakier kwiaty, jakie wianka
> Splotz na czesc Hanki.

Chopin's setting is twelve bars long, in G major and 3/8 time. It consists of the vocal line only.

Dalibor was a Czech periodical published three times a month from 1879 to 1913. The music of the Mazurka was contained in an article 'Chopin in Prague in 1829' by Dr. Otkar Hostiňsky (1847–1910), a distinguished Czech musicologist and professor of Aesthetics at the Caroline University, Prague. His article also gave Macicowski's poem, and the two letters from Chopin to his family of 19 and 26 August 1829.

MS. National Museum, Prague. When Hanka's album was re-bound some years ago, the margins were so deeply cut that almost half Chopin's autograph was removed in the operation.

40

WALTZ in D flat major, Op. 70: no. 3 (Posth.). 3 October 1829

*In some editions, e♭

Publication of Op. 70:

 A. M. Schlesinger, Berlin (4396). May 1855.

 J. Meissonnier fils, Paris (3527). February 1856.

Meissonnier's editions of the posthumous works were published without opus numbers.

The waltz was written for Konstancja Gladkowska (1810–1889), singer and friend of Chopin's youth.

The composer wrote to Titus Woyciechowski on 3 October 1829: '. . . [Konstancja] inspired me this morning to write the little waltz I am sending you.' He drew his friend's attention to bars 32–37: '. . . no one but you will know what they mean.' This reference has led to the identification of the Waltz.

Fontana's date is 1830.

MS. Lost.

40 (B)

WALTZ in A minor (sketch). (?) 1829

Unpublished

The manuscript consists of sketches for a brief prelude and the main theme.

MS. Unknown: formerly in the possession of H. Hinter-
 berger, Vienna, 1937.

41

POLONAISE in C major, for PF. and cello, Op. 3. Antonin,
20–28 October 1829

Publication:

Pietro Mechetti, Vienna (2178). Autumn 1831

Republished by:

(*a*) A. M. Schlesinger, Berlin. 1832.

(*b*) Simon Richault, Paris (3301). June 1835.

(*c*) Wessel, London (1860). April 1836.

Dedicated to Josef Merk (1795–1852), eminent Viennese cellist and professor at the Conservatoire.

The work was composed for Prince Antoine Radziwill (cello) and his daughter Wanda (piano) (see **25**). Antonin was the seat of Prince Antoine. Chopin, in a letter of 14 November 1829 to Titus Woyciechowski, refers to the Polonaise as an 'alla polacca'. He composed the Introduction later, see **52**.

Op. 3 was published by Mechetti earlier than 1833, the date usually given. This is shown by his Publisher's Number and also by the date of the Berlin republication. Mechetti published the arrangement for PF. Solo, made by Czerny, *c.* 1834, and early in 1836 he issued the work for PF. and cello *or* violin (2723), the parts for both instruments being included in the publication. The firm of Mechetti was bought by C. A. Spina, also of Vienna, in 1855.

A. M. Schlesinger's arrangement for PF. Solo appeared in 1842.

The French edition was bought from Richault by M. Schlesinger, Paris, *c.* 1841; in 1842 Schlesinger published an arrangement for PF. Solo. (3729).

Wessel's edition is entitled *La Gaîeté*. His arrangement for PF. Solo, published in October 1837 (Publisher's Number 1860), was republished *c.* 1845 as no. 50 in his series 'Le Pianiste Moderne'. In November 1838 he published an arrangement for PF. and viola, and in 1840 an arrangement for PF. and flute (arr. by J. Sedlatzek).

MS. Lost.

FOUR STUDIES from Op. 10. October to November 1829

    No. 8 in F major.
    No. 9 in F minor.
    No. 10 in A flat major.
    No. 11 in E flat major.

Publication of Op. 10:

    Probst-Kistner, Leipzig (Two parts: 1018–1019). August 1833.

    M. Schlesinger, Paris (1399). July 1833.

    Wessel, London (Book I: 960, Book II: 961). August 1833.

Dedicated to Liszt. The Paris edition carries the dedication as '. . . à son ami J. [*sic*] Liszt.'

Wessel's edition is dedicated to '. . . ses amis J. Liszt et Ferd. Hiller.' For a note on Wessel's edition, see 53.

The copyright of Op. 10, together with that of the second set of studies, Op. 25, was sold by Schlesinger at the end of 1844 to the Paris publisher Henri Lemoine.

These four studies were originally intended to be Op. 10: nos. 7–10, but were displaced by the Study in C major, the present Op. 10: no. 7.

One of these four studies was written before 20 October 1829, the others soon afterwards; this is clear from Chopin's letter to Titus Woyciechowski of 20 October 1829: 'I have composed a big *Exercise en forme* in a way of my own; I will show it to you when we meet.' Later he wrote to the same friend, on 14 November 1829: 'I have written two studies; I could play them well to you.'

No. 11, in E flat is the 'Arpeggio' Study.

MSS. (1) Nos. 8, 9 and 10: Deutsche Staatsbibliothek, Berlin. (Now in the State Collection, Warsaw.)
     (2) No. 11: Rudolf Nydahl, Stockholm.

43

CONCERTO in F minor for PF. and Orchestra, Op. 21. Autumn 1829 to early 1830

Publication:

> Breitkopf & Haertel, Leipzig (5654). April 1836.
> M. Schlesinger, Paris (1940). October 1836.
> Wessel, London (1642). November 1836.

Dedicated to Mme. la Comtesse Delphine Potocka, *née* Komar, a gifted singer, pupil and close friend of the composer.

The Larghetto was finished by September 1829; the Finale followed late in 1829 or early 1830. According to a letter from Chopin to Woyciechowski of 3 October 1829, the slow movement was inspired by Konstancja Gladkowska (see 40).

The work was called 'Second' Concerto on publication, although it is the first in order of composition. Delay in preparing the orchestral parts led to the publication of the later Concerto in E minor (53) before this one.

It was first performed privately in Chopin's home, with Kurpiński conducting, on 3 March 1830; the public performance in the National Theatre, Warsaw, followed a fortnight later.

Breitkopf & Haertel issued an arrangement for PF. Solo shortly after the first publication.

Wessel published the Concerto as Book XXXIII of his series 'Album des Pianistes de Première Force' (see 22). It was dedicated without the composer's sanction, or knowledge, to 'Mrs. Anderson'. [Mrs. Lucy Anderson (1790–1878) of Bath, PF. teacher to Queen Victoria and her children.]

The *Oxford Edition* of 1932, edited by Ganche, published for the first time a passage for the bass (Left Hand), written by Chopin for bars 43–70 of the Larghetto to be played when the movement is performed as a PF. Solo.

Karl Klindworth's arrangement was made in London in 1868 and published in 1878 by P. Jurgenson, Moscow, under the title: 'Second Concerto de Chopin, Op. 21, avec un nouvel accompagnement d'orchestre d'après la partition originale par K. Klindworth. Dédié à Fr. Liszt.' This publication became the property of Bote & Bock, Berlin.

MSS. (1) Sketches: see 25.

　　　(2) Chopin Institute, Warsaw (from Breitkopf & Haertel). The PF. part only in the composer's hand.

44

WALTZ in E major. 1829

Publication:

　　W. Chaberski, Cracow (No Publisher's Number). 1871.
　　Republished by:
　　Gebethner & Wolff, Warsaw (. . .). 1877.

The date given for this Waltz in Louise's list is 1830. Its publication by Chaberski is referred to by Szulc in his book on Chopin, 1873.

MS. Lost.

45

MAZURKA in A minor, Op. 70: no. 2 (first version). 1829

Publication:

> Breitkopf & Haertel, Leipzig, in a supplement to their
> *Gesamtausgabe* of Chopin's works ('Klavierbibliothek':
> 21,183 III). 1902.
>
> F. Hoesick, Warsaw. 1902.

This version of the Mazurka was written in Emily
Elsner's Album. It has a short Introduction (8 bars) in A
major, marked *Duda* (=bagpipe). There are other details
which differ from the final version in Op. 7 (**61**); the chief of
these is at bars 29–32, where the first version has:

MS. Emily Elsner's Album: destroyed.

46

WALTZ in E flat major. 1829–1830

Publication:

> Breitkopf & Haertel, Leipzig, in a supplement to their
> *Gesamtausgabe* of Chopin's works ('Klavierbibliothek',
> 23,183 I). 1902.

The date for the Waltz is given in Louise's list. The
publication took place after the discovery of a copy in Emily
Elsner's Album (see **21**).

MSS. (1) The copy in the Chopin family papers: lost.
      (2) Emily Elsner's Album: destroyed.

47

SONG for voice and PF., Op. 74: no. 10. Spring 1830

'Wojak' ('Rży mój gniady')

'The Warrior' ('My bay horse neighs').

(A flat major)

German title: 'Der Reiter vor der Schlacht'.

Text: Stefan Witwicki.

Publication:

A. Kocipiński, Kiev (44). 1856. Probably a re-issue of an anonymous edition from this firm in 1837.

For details of the publication of Op. 74, see **32**.

MSS. (1) Rough draft: private possession in the U.S.A.

(2) Emily Elsner's Album: destroyed.

(3) Maria Wodzińska's Album: State Collection, Warsaw.

(4) Fair copy: Artur Rubinstein.

48

SONG for voice and PF., Op. 74: no. 6. Spring 1830

'Precz z moich oczu!' ('Precz z moich oczu! posłuchani odrazu!').

'Out of my sight!' ('Out of my sight').

(F minor-A flat major)

German title: 'Mir aus den Augen!'

Text: Adam Mickiewicz.

For details of the publication of Op. 74, see **32**.

MSS. (1) Emily Elsner's Album: destroyed.

    (2) Maria Wodzińska's Album: State Collection, Warsaw.

    (3) Fair copy: State Collection, Warsaw (lost in 1939).

49

NOCTURNE in C sharp minor (*Lento con gran espressione*). Spring 1830

Publication:

    M. Leitgeber, Poznań (M.L. 18). 5 January 1875.

    Republished by:

    E. Ascherberg, London (971). 1894.

    This publication was edited by Natalie Janotha, after the reproduction in facsimile of MS. (3) below, in the *Echo Muzyczne*, Warsaw, 1894.

Leitgeber published the Nocturne with three mazurkas (**31** and **16**), with a preface by M. A. Szulc. It was entitled: *Trzy Mazury i Adagio utwory młodisci Fryderyka Chopina* ('Three Mazurkas and Adagio. Juvenilia of Frédéric Chopin'). *Adagio* was a generic term for any slow movement: the tempo was printed as *Lento con gran espressione*.

On Brahms's copy of this publication, in the possession of Antony van Hoboken, Ascona, he has crossed out the Adagio and added 'bleibt weg' ('leave out'). This is the reason for its omission from the Breitkopf & Haertel *Gesamtausgabe*. Brahms also crossed out the preface by Szulc.

At the head of Leitgeber's publication of the Adagio appear the words: 'Siostrze Ludwice dła wprawy, nim się zabierze do mego drugiego Koncertu' ('For my sister Louise to play, before she practises my second concerto.') Chopin sent a copy of the nocturne to his family from Vienna in 1830, written in minute writing, in one of his letters, and may have indicated there that it was for his sister. But this letter was destroyed in the events at the Zamojski Palace in 1863, and there is no means of substantiating this very dubious inscription.[1]

In Poland the work is sometimes called the 'Reminiscence' Nocturne, because of its self-quotations from the Second Concerto (in F minor) and from the song 'Życzenie' ('The Wish'). The title was first given to the facsimile reproduction of MS. (3) in the Warsaw *Echo Muzyczne* (see above).

MSS. Three of the four autograph manuscripts of this Nocturne listed below are extant (the whereabouts of one of them is at present unknown), but they do not agree in detail. They are given here in the probable order of composition.

(1) 1 leaf, both sides written on. Unpublished. A facsimile reproduction is given in *Chopin in der Heimat*, Cracow, 1955. Arthur Hedley, London.

(2) Written in a letter of 1830 from Vienna and recorded in Louise's list. Destroyed in 1863, but previously copied by the family. This copy was used as the basis for Leitgeber's publication.

(3) 1 leaf, one side written on. A facsimile reproduction was given in the 1894 *Echo Muzyczne*, and

[1] See *Monthly Musical Record*, November to December 1956.

again on the cover of Ascherberg's edition (above). Unknown.[1]

(4) 2 leaves, three sides written on. The copy made by Chopin in 1836 for Maria Wodzińska. It was written in a small album, the whole reproduced in facsimile by Breitkopf & Haertel 1910 (see 51). The first page was again reproduced by this firm in their *Das Musikbuch*, 1913, page 66. The introductory bar of this version is as follows:

The whole of MS. (4) was again reproduced by Binental in his *Documents and Souvenirs of Chopin*, Warsaw, 1930. Chopin Institute, Warsaw.

50

TWO SONGS for voice and PF., Op. 74: nos. 4 and 7. 1830

No. 4. 'Hulanka' ('Szynkareczko').
      'Merrymaking' ('Serving maid, take care').

(E flat major)

No. 7. 'Poseł' ('Błysło ranne ziółko').
      'The Envoy' ('The early sun broke forth').

(F major)

German titles: 'Bacchanale' and 'Der Bote'.
Texts of both songs: Stefan Witwicki.

[1] Although this manuscript is reproduced as a Chopin autograph it is almost certainly not in the composer's hand.

For details of the publication of Op. 74, see 32.

Liszt transcribed no. 4, 'Hulanka', for PF. Solo. 'Posel' is mentioned by Witwicki in his letter to Chopin of 6 July 1831.

MSS. (1) No. 7, 'Posel': State Collection, Warsaw.

   (2) Both songs: Emily Elsner's Album: destroyed.

   (3) Both songs: Maria Wodzińska's Album: State Collection, Warsaw.

51

SONG for voice and PF. 1830

  'Czary' ('To sa czary, pewnoczary!').
  'Charms' ('This charms, so surely charms!').

(D minor)

German title: 'Liebeszauber'.
Text: Stefan Witwicki.

E

Publication:

Breitkopf & Haertel, Leipzig. 1910.

The publication was a facsimile reproduction of the Album which Chopin had written and sent to Maria Wodzińska in 1836. It was entitled:

Maria. Ein Liebesidyll in Tönen.
Chopin an Maria Wodzińska.

The edition contained a preface and appendix by Kornelia Parnas, who had received the album from a niece of Maria Wodzińska.

Costallat, Paris. 1911.

This was a similar facsimile reproduction, with French translations of the songs by Gaston Knosp. It was entitled:

Maria. Une idylle d'amour en musique.
Chopin à Maria Wodzińska.

The first true publication was in vol. XVII of the Polish 'Complete Works' of Chopin, Warsaw, 1954.

The last stanza in Chopin's autograph (MS. no. 3 below) is not found in Witwicki's collected poems (*Biblical poems, pastoral songs and sundry verses*, Paris, 1836), indicating that the composer knew the poems in a manuscript version which differed from the final text.

'Czary' was rejected by Fontana from Op. 74 as being, in his opinion, unworthy of Chopin.

MSS. (1) Fair copy: State Collection, Warsaw.
     (2) Emily Elsner's Album: destroyed.
     (3) Maria Wodzińska's Album: State Collection, Warsaw.

INTRODUCTION in C major to the Polonaise for PF. and cello, Op. 3. April 1830

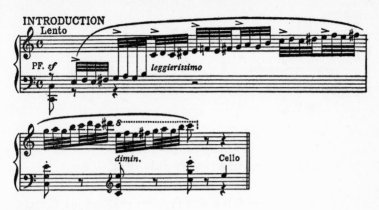

Publication: see **41**.

Chopin wrote to Woyciechowski on 10 April 1830: 'My Polonaise with the cello, to which I added an *Adagio* Introduction specially for Kaczyński. . . .' The whole work was performed by the composer with Kaczyński at a soirée in Lewicki's house in Warsaw in April 1830.

The MS. was deposited with Mechetti in July 1831 by Chopin himself before he left Vienna for Paris. For the Polonaise, see **41**.

MS. Lost.

53

CONCERTO in E minor, for PF. and Orchestra, Op. 11. April to August 1830

Publication:

>Probst-Kistner, Leipzig (1020–1022). September 1833.
>
>M. Schlesinger, Paris (1343). July 1833.
>
>Wessel, London (1086). May 1834.

Dedicated to Friedrich Kalkbrenner (1788–1849), German composer, pianist and teacher: resident in Paris.

The first two movements were finished by April 1830; the whole work by 21 August 1830. Delay in copying the orchestral parts of the PF. Concerto in F minor led to this Concerto, the second in order of composition, being published first.

The Concerto was performed by the composer privately on 22 September 1830, and publicly in the Town Hall, Warsaw, on 11 October 1830. The first performance is sometimes erroneously stated to have taken place at the house of Augustus Klengel in Dresden on 23 September 1830.

Kistner's three editions are (*a*) the original form, (*b*) the orchestral part arranged for a second piano, (*c*) the whole work arranged for PF. Solo.

Wessel published the Concerto as Book XXIV of his series 'Album des Pianistes de Première Force' (see 22). He claimed that it was 'edited and fingered' by Chopin's pupil 'I. [*sic*] Fontana.' The same claim was made for the Studies, Op. 10. There is, actually, a possibility that Chopin did authorise Fontana in the matter.

Karl Taussig's arrangement was published by Ries & Erler, Berlin, in 1866, under the title: *Grosses Konzert in e-moll, Op. 11*, Bearbeitet von Karl Taussig. (P.N. 2047).

MS. Lost.

54

THREE NOCTURNES, Op. 9. Spring 1830–1831

No. 1 in B flat minor.
No. 2 in E flat major.
No. 3 in B major.

Publication:

Probst-Kistner, Leipzig (995). December 1832.
M. Schlesinger, Paris (1287). Early 1833.
Wessel, London (nos. 1 and 2: 916; no. 3: 917). June 1833.

Dedicated to Marie Pleyel (1811–1875), wife of Camille Pleyel.

The first few bars of No. 2, in E flat major, were written on a card to Maria Wodzińska by Chopin and dated 22 September 1835. On the other side of the card he wrote 'Soyez heureuse'. In this short extract the composer has barred the music as if it were in 6/8! (State Collection, Warsaw).

Op. 9 was published in France before Opp. 6 and 7.

The English edition, entitled *Murmures de la Seine*, was also published before Opp. 6 and 7, and carried no opus number. Wessel later re-issued the work as nos. 66 (1 and 2) and 67 (3) of his series 'L'amateur Pianiste'.

MS. No. 2, in E flat major: State Collection, Warsaw.

55

TWO NOCTURNES from Op. 15. Spring 1830–1831[1]

No. 1 in F major.
No. 2 in F sharp major.

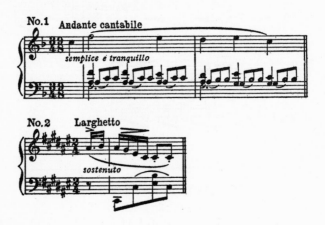

Publication of Op. 15:

Breitkopf & Haertel, Leipzig (5502). December 1833.
M. Schlesinger, Paris (1529). January 1834.
Wessel, London (1093). May 1834.

Dedicated to Ferdinand Hiller (1811–1885), German composer and pianist, resident in Paris 1828–1835. A copy of the Paris edition, in the possession of Antony van Hoboken, Ascona, is inscribed by Chopin, 'À son ami, Ferdinand, F. F. Chopin, Fevrier 1834.'

---

[1] In the opinion of Arthur Hedley, the three nocturnes of Op. 15 were composed later, in fact, after Chopin's arrival in Paris.

Breitkopf & Haertel sent copies of the publication to the composer in December 1833.

Schlesinger's publication is in the form of an Album Supplement to his *Gazette Musicale* of January 1834.

The English edition was entitled *Les Zephirs*. Wessel later re-issued the work as no. 68 of his series 'L'amateur Pianiste.'

For Op. 15 : no. 3, the Nocturne in G minor, see 79.

MS. Lost.

56

WALTZ in E minor. (? May) 1830

Publication:

> J. Kauffmann, Warsaw (. . .). 1868.
> B. Schott's Sons, Mainz (19,551). 1868.

Schott's Sons issued an arrangement for PF. Duet shortly after the publication of the Waltz.

Chaberski, Cracow, published the E minor Waltz in 1871, shortly after his publication of the Waltz in E major (see 44).

This may be the waltz referred to by Chopin in his letter of 15 May 1830 to Woyciechowski: 'I meant to send you a new waltz to amuse you, but you shall have it next week.' (But see 44).

MS. Lost. Occasional fingering in the first edition suggests that Kauffmann used Chopin's autograph.

57

Two Studies from Op. 10. (? summer) 1830

No. 5 in G flat major.
No. 6 in E flat minor.

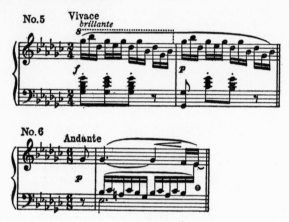

For details of the publication of Op. 10, see 42.

No. 5, in G flat major, is the 'Black Key' Study; the name is partly authorised by Chopin himself (see his letter to Julian Fontana of 25 April 1839).

MSS. Both Studies: Deutsche Staatsbibliothek, Berlin (now in the State Collection, Warsaw).

Lost work of 1830:

Waltz in A flat major. (? December)

The Waltz may be the one referred to by Chopin in his letter of 21 December 1830 from Vienna to his family: 'I wanted to send you a waltz I have composed, but it is late now; you shall have it afterwards.' It is given in Louise's list, with the date, and so was evidently a possession of the Chopin family c. 1854.

GRAND POLONAISE in E flat major, for PF. and Orchestra, Op. 22. September 1830 to July 1831

Publication:

Breitkopf & Haertel, Leipzig (5709). August 1836.
M. Schlesinger, Paris (1926). August 1836.
Wessel, London (1643). August 1836.

Dedicated to Mme. la Baronne d'Est, sister of Pauline de Noailles, pupil of Chopin.

In a letter of 18 September 1830 to Woyciechowski, Chopin wrote: 'I have begun a Polonaise with the orchestra.' The work was first performed in Paris on 26 April 1835 at the 'Société des Concerts du Conservatoire', in François Habeneck's 'Benefit Concert' (Habeneck was the founder of the concerts).

The Introduction—*Andante Spianato*—was composed later, but published at the same time as the Polonaise (see 88).

On the French edition Mori & Lavenu are given as the English publishers: this is an error, and probably represents an unsuccessful bid for the publication of the work. Wessel published the work as Book XXXIV of the 'Album des Pianistes de Première Force' (see 22). His arrangement for PF. Solo appeared in July 1838.

MS. State Collection, Warsaw.

59

Two Studies from Op. 10. Late autumn 1830

    No. 1 in C major.
    No. 2 in A minor.

For details of the publication of Op. 10, see 42.

MSS. (1) First writing down of no. 2, in A minor, signed by the composer and called 'Étude': Rudolf Nydahl, Stockholm.

     (2) Fair copy of both studies, entitled 'Exercise 1 and 2', the second one dated 'November 2, 1830': Deutsche Staatsbibliothek, Berlin (now in the State Collection, Warsaw).

60

Four Mazurkas, Op. 6. Vienna, late 1830

    No. 1 in F sharp minor.
    No. 2 in C sharp minor.
    No. 3 in E major.
    No. 4 in E flat minor.

Publication:

Probst-Kistner, Leipzig (996). December 1832.
M. Schlesinger, Paris (1341). August 1833.
Wessel, London (958). August 1833.

Dedicated to Mlle. la Comtesse Pauline Plater. The Plater family were exiled compatriots and close friends of the composer.

These are possibly the mazurkas referred to by Chopin in his letter of 21 December 1830 to his parents: 'I don't send the mazurkas because they are not copied yet; they are not for dancing.'

Breitkopf & Haertel, in their 'Thematic Catalogue' of the works of Chopin (Leipzig, *c.* 1856, a later, revised edition of the 1852 issue of the 'Catalogue'), include under 'Doubtful Compositions' an arrangement of No. 1, in F sharp minor, with an Introduction in A major, dedicated to Dr. H. Mumm. This mazurka was published by Kistner *c.* 1853.

The English edition of these mazurkas, and those of Opp. 7, 17, 24 and 30, were entitled *Souvenirs de la Pologne*. Wessel re-issued Op. 6 later as no. 8 in his series 'L'amateur Pianiste' (*c.* 1846).

The French edition of Op. 6 included, as a fifth mazurka, Op. 7: no. 5, in C major. For this edition, see also **25**.

MSS. (1) No. 2, in C sharp minor, first sketch (about 36 bars): Musée Adam Mickiewicz, Bibliothèque Polonaise, Paris. It was given to the poet's son, Ladislas, by Fontana, who has added the date of Chopin's death.

  (2) Fair copy of No. 2: Rudolf Nydahl, Stockholm.

(3) No. 3, in E major, in an autograph album: Rudolf Kallir and Walter Benjamin, U.S.A.

61

FIVE MAZURKAS, Op. 7. Vienna, 1830–1831

No. 1 in B flat major.
No. 2 in A minor (2nd version).
No. 3 in F minor.
No. 4 in A flat major (comp. 1824).
No. 5 in C major.

Publication:

Probst-Kistner, Leipzig (997). December 1832.
M. Schlesinger, Paris (1342). August 1833.
Wessel, London (959). August 1833.

Dedicated to M. Johns of New Orleans. Johns, whose first name seems to be unknown, was commended by Chopin to Hiller as 'a distinguished amateur of New Orleans'.

For the first version of No. 2, in A minor, see **45**. For particulars of No. 4, in A flat major, see **7**.

In Schlesinger's first edition, No. 5, in C major, was omitted. See **60**.

Wessel re-issued Op. 7 as no. 9 in his series 'L'amateur Pianiste'.

Friedrich Kalkbrenner's 'Variations brillantes pour le PF. sur une Mazurka de Chopin', Op. 120, is based on No. 1, in B flat major.

MSS. (1) No. 1, in B flat major: Rudolf Floersheim, Muzzano-Lugano (Louis Koch Collection). A facsimile of this MS. is given in Adolf Weissmann's *Chopin*, Berlin, 1912; it was reproduced, as were all of Weissmann's facsimile reproductions, from a bookseller's catalogue, in this case from the catalogue of C. G. Boerner, Leipzig, May 1908. It is an earlier version than the published one and contains minor variants.

(2) No. 3, in F minor: (*a*) a copy signed 'Vienna. F. F. Chopin. 20.6.1831'. Rudolf Floersheim, Muzzano-Lugano (Louis Koch Collection). (*b*) a copy dated 'Vienna. 20.7.1831.' Presented by its owner, Louis Koch, in 1930, to the Russian cellist 'J.Pl.' (?). (*c*) a copy undated: present whereabouts unknown. It was formerly in the Kistner archives, Leipzig. There is a facsimile reproduction in the German edition of Niecks's biography: *Chopin als Mensch und Musiker*, Leipzig, 1889.

(3) No. 4, in A flat major: see **7**.

62

Wᴀʟᴛᴢ in E flat major, Op. 18. Vienna, 1831

Publication:

> Breitkopf & Haertel, Leipzig (5545). July 1834.
> M. Schlesinger, Paris (1599). June 1834.
> Wessel, London (1157). July 1834.

Dedicated to Mlle. Laura Horsford. Her name appears on early editions (not Wessel's), up to *c.* 1855, as 'Harsford'. It was corrected from her sister's name. She was the daughter of General George Horsford (see **80**), and later became Mrs. Laura Lowther.

The composer sent a copy of this publication to Maria Wodzińska (see **95**). In his letter of 18 July 1834 to her brother Feliks Wodziński, Chopin wrote: 'I take the liberty of sending to my estimable colleague, Mlle. Maria, a little waltz which I have just published.' He inscribed the printed copy with the words: 'To Mlle. Maria with respects from her former teacher.' ('Hommage à Mlle. M. W. de la part de son ancient professeur F. F. Chopin. 18 jui. 1834.'). The month, which could be 'juin' or 'juillet', has been wrongly interpreted as 'juin' (June). That it is, in fact, 'July', is clear from the beginning of the letter above (and see **86**). The inscribed copy is in the State Collection, Warsaw. Maria had sent Chopin a set of variations composed by herself.

The copyright of the work was sold by Schlesinger to Henri Lemoine, Paris, at the end of 1844.

The English edition was entitled *Invitation pour la Danse* and the waltz became widely known in England as 'L'Invitation'. Wessel later re-issued the waltz as no. 28 in his series 'L'amateur Pianiste', and again in a *Collection of German Waltzes*.

MSS. (1) State Collection, Warsaw.
(2) Mariemont Museum, Belgium.

63

THREE SONGS for voice and PF., Op. 74: nos. 3, 15 and 16. Vienna, 1831

No. 3 'Smutna Rzeka' ('Rzeko z cudzoziemców strony')
'The sad stream' ('A stream flowing from foreign
parts')

(F sharp minor)

German title: 'Trübe Wellen'.
Text: Stefan Witwicki.

MS. Lost.

No. 15 'Narzeczony' (Wiatr zaszumiał...')
'The Bridegroom' ('The wind rose...')

(E minor)

German title: 'Die Heimkehr'.
Text: Stefan Witwicki.

MS. State Collection, Warsaw.

No. 16 'Piosńka Litewska' ('Bardzo raniuchno')
'Lithuanian Song' ('Very early in the morning')

(F major)

German title: 'Lithuanisches Lied'.
Text: Ludwika Osińskiego.

MSS. (1) Musée Adam Mickiewicz, Bibliothèque Polonaise,
Paris (first sketch).
(2) Memorial Library of Music, Stanford University,
California (see **12**) (fair copy).
(3) Maria Wodzińska's Album: State Collection,
Warsaw.

For details of the publication of Op. 74, see **32**.

64

WALTZ in A minor, Op. 34: no. 2. Vienna, 1831

Publication:

Breitkopf & Haertel, Leipzig (6033). December 1838.
M. Schlesinger, Paris (2716). December 1838.
Wessel, London (2281). December 1838.

Dedicated to Mme. la Baronne C. d'Ivri.
For the other two waltzes of Op. 34: no. 1, in A flat
major, see **94**, no. 2, in F major, see **118**.

MSS. (1) Dated 'Vienna 1831': Arthur Hedley, London.
(2) Fragment (title page): Society of Music, Warsaw.

65

SCHERZO no. 1, in B minor, Op. 20. Vienna, May to June 1831; revised Paris, 1832

Publication:

Breitkopf & Haertel, Leipzig (5599). March 1835.

M. Schlesinger, Paris (1832). February (–April) 1835.

Wessel, London (1492). August 1835.

Dedicated to M. Thomas Albrecht, wine merchant, attaché to the Saxon Legation in Paris, and one of the composer's warmest friends.

The Trio (not so called by Chopin) in B major is based on the Polish Christmas folk-tune 'Lulajże Jezuniu' ('Lullaby, little Jesus'):

The English edition is entitled *Le Banquet Infernal*. Wessel re-issued the work later as no. 56 in his series 'L'amateur Pianiste'.

The French edition was presented first as an exclusive supplement for subscribers to Schlesinger's journal *Gazette Musicale*. It was on sale normally two months later.

MS. Lost.

BALLADE no. 1, in G minor, Op. 23. Vienna, sketched May to June 1831: completed Paris, 1835

Publication:

> Breitkopf & Haertel, Leipzig (5706). June 1836.
> M. Schlesinger, Paris (1928). July 1836.
> Wessel, London (1644). August 1836.

Dedicated to M. le Baron de Stockhausen, Hanoverian Ambassador to France (father of Elisabet Herzogenberg, the friend of Brahms).

The disputed E flat in the tenor part of bar 7 is unmistakable in MS. (1) below, reproduced in the *Revue Musicale*, Paris, December 1931.

Breitkopf & Haertel published the Ballade separately, but also, at the same time, included it in an *Album Musical*, containing a miscellany of songs and PF. pieces by Loewe, Liszt, Spohr, Mendelssohn etc. In this *Album* Chopin's work was entitled 'Ballade ohne Worte'.

The work is sometimes called the 'Polish' Ballade. The English edition was entitled *Ballade ohne Worte*, or *La Favorite Ballade*. Wessel re-issued the work as no. 69 in his series 'L'amateur Pianiste'.

Schumann's remark: '. . . sein genialischtes (nicht genialstes) Werk' was written of this Ballade.

MSS. (1) Mme. R. Calmann-Levy, Paris (incomplete MS.).
(2) Gregor Piatigorsky, U.S.A.

67

STUDY in C minor, Op. 10: no. 12. (?) September 1831

For details of publication of Op. 10, see 42.

The work is the so-called 'Revolutionary' Study and is supposed to have been inspired by the downfall of Warsaw in September 1831, the news of which reached the composer at Stuttgart. There is no particle of evidence for this most firmly entrenched legend in the Chopin literature, and as with other nicknamed works of the composer its attributed date is therefore not to be relied on.

MSS. (1) Rudolf Nydahl, Stockholm.
(2) Nine bars (nos. 9–17), written in the Album of George Sand, and with the indication *appassionato*: Nicolas Rauch, Geneva, November 1957.

68

STUDY in C major, Op. 10: no. 7. Spring 1832

For details of the publication of Op. 10, see 42.

The piece was placed seventh in the original opus.

MS. The Ernest Schelling Collection, U.S.A. (two pages).

69

CONTRABASS PART to a three-part Canon in B minor by Mendelssohn. 16 April 1832

Mendelssohn called his Canon 'à 3', but his bass part is in strict canon with the three upper parts. Chopin's addition is not to be taken seriously: a free, florid parody written in the empty bars of Mendelssohn's bass stave.

The MS. contains this remark by Mendelssohn: 'Contra basso libro composti di Scopino [i.e. Chopin]. La basso est à vous. Felix Mendelssohn-Bartholdy. Paris, 16.4.32.'

The page is reproduced in facsimile in Binental's *Documents and Souvenirs of Chopin*, Warsaw, 1930.

MS. Originally in the possession of Mme. Laura Ciechom-ska, Warsaw, whose collection was destroyed in 1939.

70

GRAND DUO in E major, on themes from Meyerbeer's *Robert le Diable*, for PF. and cello. Published without opus number. Early 1832

Publication:

A. M. Schlesinger, Berlin (1777). July 1833.
M. Schlesinger, Paris (1376). 6 July 1833.
Wessel, London (1085). December 1833.

The work was composed in collaboration with Auguste Joseph Franchomme (see **160**). In his letter of 12 December 1831 to Woyciechowski, Chopin wrote: '. . . Schlesinger . . . has engaged me to write something on themes from *Robert le Diable*, which he has bought from Meyerbeer for 24,000 francs.'

Amongst themes used, the chief ones are:

(*a*) the 'Romanza', Act I,
(*b*) the Chorus 'Non v'e pieta', Act I,
(*c*) the Terzetto 'Le mie cure, ancor dal cielo', Act V.

Robert le Diable was first performed at the Paris Opéra on 21 November 1831.

The Duo was later arranged by Chopin and Franchomme as a PF. Duet and this was published by A. M. Schlesinger (P.N. 2238) in 1838; it was given erroneously the opus number '15'.

Wessel called this Duo on publication 'Opus 12', substituting it for the real Op. 12, the variations on a theme from Hérold (see **80**).

A PF. Duet arrangement was also published by Schlesinger in Paris in February 1839 (P. N. 2799) and called 'Op. 15'.

The Duo concludes in A major.

MS. Conservatoire, Paris.

71

MAZURKA in D major. 1832

Publication:

> Breitkopf & Haertel, Leipzig (*Gesamtausgabe*, vol. XIII, no. 7). January 1880.

This is a considerably revised version of the Mazurka in D major, of 1829 (see 31).

MS. Lost.

72

ALLEGRO DE CONCERT in A major, Op. 46. Sketched in 1832, revised and completed in May 1841

Publication:

> Breitkopf & Haertel, Leipzig (6651). December 1841.
> M. Schlesinger, Paris (3481). November 1841.
> Wessel, London (5298). March 1842.

Dedicated to Friederike Müller, a favourite pupil of Chopin, who became an eminent Austrian pianist. She married Johann Baptiste Streicher, the Viennese pianoforte manufacturer. Her letter of thanks to the composer, sent from Vienna, is dated 21 December 1841.

It seems fairly clear that the work was originally conceived as a PF. concerto, the material possibly dating from as early as 1830 when Chopin, in Vienna, had discussed the composition of a concerto for two pianofortes to be played by himself and his friend (and schoolfellow) Thomas Nidecki. Either this, or fresh, material was worked on in 1832 for the first movement of a PF. concerto. His father mentioned this projected work in a letter of 1834, and wrote again on 11 April 1835: 'You don't mention whether you have finished your third concerto'—words which probably refer to this proposed work. The music was taken up once more in the spring of 1841 after a promise to Friederike Müller to compose a concert piece for her. The 'Allegro de Concert' is thus a pastiche of early work in which the original *soli* and *tutti* passages are still distinguishable. That the composer always thought of it as a concerto is clear from his letter to Fontana of 16 October 1841, in which he wrote of it by that name. (See **142**).

An arrangement of the piece for PF. and Orchestra, by Jean Louis Nicode (1835–1919), a pupil of Kullak, and like the composer himself, a Pole of French extraction, was published by Breitkopf & Haertel in 1880. He added 79 spurious bars.

MSS. (1) Chopin Institute, Warsaw (originally in the possession of Breitkopf & Haertel, and containing Chopin's dedication to 'Mlle. F. Müller (de Vienne)'.

(2) The MS. in the possession of the Heinemann Foundation, New York, is a fair copy made by Fontana, and not an autograph of Chopin's. (14 pages).

73

Mazurka in B flat major. 24 June 1832

Publication:

Lamus (a periodical), no. 2, Lwow. 1909.

The work, thirty-two bars long, was composed for Mme.

Alexandra Wolowska, wife of 'Wolowski, the deputy', as he is called by Chopin's friends. It was written in her album, which was discovered in the posthumous papers of the Kátýl family, Polish refugees living in Paris, by Dr. Stanilas Lam.

There is a facsimile reproduction of the *Lamus* publication in Maria Mirska's book *Szłakiem Chopina*, Warsaw, 1935.

MS. Jasieński Museum, Lwow.

74

STUDY in E major, Op. 10: no. 3. 25 August 1832

For details of the publication of Op. 10, see **42**.

The study was originally marked *vivace*, and there was no later direction *poco più animato*. The tempo was subsequently changed to *Lento ma non troppo*.

MSS. (1) First version with several important variants, dated 'Paris, 25 August 1832': Alfred Cortot, Lausanne.

(2) Fair copy: Deutsche Staatsbibliothek, Berlin (now in the State Collection, Warsaw). This is marked *Vivace ma non troppo*.

(MS. (1) was presented, together with Op. 10: no. 4, in C sharp minor, to Friederike Müller by the composer. See **72** and **75**.)

75

STUDY in C sharp minor, Op. 10: no. 4. August 1832

For details of the publication of Op. 10, see 42.

MS. Dated 'Paris, August 1832': Rudolf Floersheim, Muzzano-Lugano, Switzerland (The Louis Koch Collection). This MS., together with that of Op. 10: no. 3, was presented by the composer to Friederike Müller in April 1841 (see 74 and 72).

76

INTRODUCTION AND RONDO in E flat major, Op. 16. 1832

Publication:

    Breitkopf & Haertel, Leipzig (5525). March 1834.

    M. Schlesinger, Paris (1703). March 1834.

    Wessel, London (1143). July 1834.

Dedicated 'à son élève, Mlle. Caroline Hartmann.' Caroline Hartmann (1808–1834), daughter of a cotton manufacturer of Münster, and admired as a child prodigy by Spohr, was a pupil of Chopin and Liszt. She afterwards became a well-known pianist and composer.

The Introduction (*Andante*) is in C minor.

Wessel's edition appeared under the title: 'Rondoletto sur

le Cavatina de *L'Italiana in Algeri*'. This claim is, of course, without foundation. His PF. Duet arrangement, published in October 1837, was called *Rondo Élégante*. He re-issued the work later as no. 24 of his series 'L'amateur Pianiste'.

Breitkopf & Haertel's edition wrongly gives Pleyel, Paris, as the publisher of the French edition.

MS. Lost.

77

FOUR MAZURKAS, Op. 17. 1832–1833

    No. 1 in B flat major.
    No. 2 in E minor.
    No. 3 in A flat major.
    No. 4 in A minor.

Publication:

    Breitkopf & Haertel, Leipzig (5527). March 1834.
    M. Schlesinger, Paris (1704). March 1834.
    Wessel, London (1144). June 1834.

Dedicated to Mme. Lina Freppa, a teacher of singing. She was born in Naples of French extraction, separated from her husband and resident in Paris. She was a friend of Chopin and Bellini, and a favourite with both composers.

Mazurka No. 4, in A minor, was first sketched in 1824 (see 8).

Wessel's edition is dedicated to Mme. Lina Treppa [*sic*]. He re-issued the work as no. 27 in his series 'L'amateur Pianiste'.

The Breitkopf & Haertel edition wrongly gives Pleyel, Paris, as the publisher of the French edition.

MS. Lost.

78

SIX STUDIES from Op. 25. 1832–1834

    No. 4 in A minor.
    No. 5 in E minor.
    No. 6 in G sharp minor.
    No. 8 in D flat major.
    No. 9 in G flat major.
    No. 10 in B minor.

Publication of Op. 25:

 Breitkopf & Haertel, Leipzig (Two parts: 5832–3). October 1837.

 M. Schlesinger, Paris (2427). October 1837.

 Wessel, London (Two parts: Book I, 1832; Book II, 1833). October 1837.

Dedicated to Marie, Comtesse d'Agoult (1805–1876), French authoress ('Daniel Stern'), mother, by Liszt, of Cosima, Wagner's second wife.

 No. 6, in G sharp minor, is the 'Thirds' Study; No. 8, in D flat major, is the 'Sixths' Study; No. 9, in G flat minor, is the 'Butterfly-wings' Study; No. 10, in B minor, is the 'Octaves' Study

 Schlesinger's copyright was sold to Henri Lemoine, Paris, in early 1842 (Lemoine's P.N. is 2776).

 Wessel's edition numbers the studies of Op. 25 as if they

continued the series in Op. 10, i.e. Book I contains nos. 13–18 and Book II nos. 19–24.

MSS. (1) Complete manuscript of Op. 25: Chopin Institute, Warsaw (originally with Breitkopf & Haertel).

(2) Nos. 4, 9 and 10: Lost, formerly with Edouard Frank.

(3) No. 4, in A minor: Bibliothèque de l'Opéra, Paris.

79

NOCTURNE in G minor, Op. 15: no. 3. 1833

For details of the publication of Op. 15, see 55.

The Album supplement to Schlesinger's *Gazette Musicale*, containing the three nocturnes of Op. 15, was sent by Chopin to his sister Louise early in 1834, that is, soon after its publication. This Album also contained treatments by various composers contemporary with Chopin of the 'Ronde' theme from Hérold's *Ludovic* on which he himself had written variations (see next). It was called *Album des Pianistes, 7th Year* and had a portrait of Chopin, by J. Vigneron, as a frontispiece. Louise's copy is now in the possession of Arthur Hedley, London.

The story that Chopin wrote on the MS. of this G minor Nocturne 'After a performance of *Hamlet*' is almost certainly an invention.

MS. Lost.

INTRODUCTION AND VARIATIONS in B flat major, on the 'Ronde' from Hérold's *Ludovic*, Op. 12. Summer 1833

Publication:

    Breitkopf & Haertel, Leipzig (5495). November 1833.

    M. Schlesinger, Paris (1499). January 1834.

    Cramer, Addison & Beale, London (. . .). 1834.

Dedicated to Mlle. Emma Horsford, a pupil of Chopin, and the daughter of General George Horsford, sometime Lieutenant-Governor of the Bermudas. She later became Mrs. Emma Appleyard. (See **62**).

Hérold died while working on *Ludovic* and the opera was completed by Fromental Halévy. The first performance of the opera took place in Paris on 16 May 1833. The theme is from Act I, no. 2, the 'Ronde favori':

        Je vends des scapulaires,

        Et de pieux rosaires . . .

for soprano solo and chorus. The key is the same as in the opera. The introduction—*Allegro maestoso*—is followed by four variations.

The theme was also made the basis of variations, fantasias and so forth by Johann Peter Pixis, Franz Hünten and

Henri Herz, and their work published in the Album supplement containing Chopin's Op. 15 (see previous item).

The *Ludovic* Variations were not included in Wessel's English edition; instead the 'Grand Duo Concertante' for PF. and cello (70), which has no opus number, was substituted, and called 'Op. 12'.

The German edition was the first publication by Breitkopf & Haertel of a work by Chopin.

The French edition was announced as early as July 1833.

MS. Lost.

81

INTRODUCTION AND BOLERO in A minor and major, Op. 19. 1833

INTRODUCTION

Publication:

    C. F. Peters, Leipzig (2505). October 1834.
    Prillip, Paris (237: see note below). Early 1835.
    Wessel, London (1491). August 1835.

Dedicated to Mlle. la Comtesse Emilie de Flahaut.

The Introduction is in C major.

The English edition was entitled *Souvenir d'Andalousie*. It was issued directly as no. 54 of the series 'L'amateur Pianiste'. The Paris publisher is given by Wessel as Phillip, but the variants in the spelling of this name, even in Paris itself, are very numerous.

Prillip's first edition has no Publisher's Number; it was

added to later editions. He was a successor to Pleyel, Paris, acquiring part of Pleyel's business in 1834. The French edition was reviewed in the *Gazette Musicale*, 25 March 1835.

MS. Sketch (incomplete) for the first version: Conservatoire, Paris. This sketch was published in the *Journal de Musique*, Paris, no. 8, 22 July 1876, under the fictitious title 'Chanson de Zingara: Souvenir du voyage en Espagne' (see 33).

82

MAZURKA in C major. 1833

Publication:

J. Kauffmann, Warsaw (171). 1870.
B. Schott's Sons, Mainz (20,030). 1870.

This Mazurka may have been intended for the publisher Schuberth, Hamburg, who, in September 1833, advertised an *Original-Bibliothek für PF.*, to contain pieces by modern composers. Among the names is Chopin's.

MS. Lost.

83

STUDY in A minor, Op. 25 : no. 11. 1834

For details of the publication of Op. 25, see 78.

This is the 'Winter Wind' Study. The four opening bars were added later, on the suggestion of Charles A. Hoffmann.

MS. See 78.

84

'CANTABILE' in B flat major. 1834

Publication:

> *Muzyka*, nos. 4–6, Warsaw (edited by Ludwig Brońarski), 1931.

The piece, 6/8, 14 bars long, was reproduced in facsimile in the *Album von Handschriften berühmter Persönlichkeiten von Mittelalter bis zur Neuzeit*. This volume, published by Rudolf Geering, Basel, in 1925, was a collection of facsimiles of autograph *facsimiles*, in the possession of the late Karl Geigy-Hagenbach (now of his heirs) in Basel.

MS. Signed 'F. F. Chopin, Paris 1834': unknown.

85

MAZURKA in A flat major. July 1834

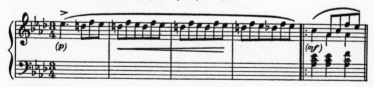

Publication:

> Gebethner & Wolff, Warsaw (edited by Maria Mirska). (6905). 1930. The edition gives a facsimile of the MS.

The manuscript carries the heading 'Paris 1834'. It was inserted in an album which had belonged to Maria Szymanowska, the celebrated Polish pianist, pupil of John Field and beloved by Goethe; she died in 1831 at St. Petersburg. The Mazurka was probably placed in the album by her daughter, Celina, who came to Paris in July 1834 to marry Adam Mickiewicz, the poet, and a friend of Chopin. There seems little doubt that the Mazurka was written for Celina Szymanowska, although there is no dedication on the manuscript.

The next facsimile reproduction was in *Die Musik*, Berlin, vol. XXIII, no. 6, March 1931. There was also a reproduction of the first page in the catalogue of the 'Frederic Chopin Exposition', arranged by the Bibliothèque Polonaise, Paris, in 1932. The whole Mazurka, forty-two bars long, was again reproduced in facsimile in *Szlakiem Chopina*, by Maria Mirska, Warsaw, 1935.

MS. Musée Adam Mickiewicz, Bibliothèque Polonaise, Paris.

86

PRELUDE in A flat. 10 July 1834

Publication:

> *Pages d'Art* (a periodical), Geneva, August 1918.
> Republished by:
>> (*a*) Henn, Geneva (244). 1919.
>> ?{(*b*) Rossignol, Paris.
>> (*c*) London & Continental Music Publishing Co., London.

The inscription on the autograph is to Pierre Wolff, and the date is 10 July 1834. Wolff (1810–1882) was a teacher of the pianoforte at the Geneva Conservatoire and a friend of Liszt. Liszt dedicated his 'Grande Valse di bravura' (composed in 1865) to him. Chopin became acquainted with Wolff through their mutual friendship with Anton Wodziński, since the Wodziński family was, at that time, living in Geneva. Chopin, in his letter of 18 July 1834 to Anton's brother, Feliks, wrote: 'So I had to wait [i.e. before answering Feliks' letter] till after the good Wolff had gone.'

The Prelude was first performed in public by E. R. Blanchet on 9 April 1919; the republication above followed this performance.

The French and English editions, though projected, were, as far as is known, never carried through.

The manuscript of the Prelude passed from Wolff to his pupil Aline Forget. It was found in the family papers by Pierre Forget, and from him passed to its present owner.

MS. Edouard Forget, Geneva.

87

FANTASIE-IMPROMPTU in C sharp minor, Op. 66 (Posth.). 1834

Publication:

   A. M. Schlesinger, Berlin (4392). May 1855.

   J. Meissonnier fils, Paris (3523). February 1856.

Meissonnier's editions of the posthumous works were published without opus numbers.

Dedicated to Mme. d'Esté. (?)

The reason why Chopin withheld this piece from publication is not known. Arthur Hedley (*Chopin*, London, 1947) suggests that it is because the theme bore too close a resemblance to Moscheles's 'Impromptu in E flat', Op. 89. This Impromptu of Moscheles was included in the Album Supplement containing Chopin's Op. 15 (see 55).

Another theory was put forward by Ernst Oster, 1947, in which Chopin is said to have derived his theme from the finale of Beethoven's Op. 27: no. 2, the 'Moonlight' Sonata, and would, therefore, not publish it.

The date is according to Fontana. It has been suggested that he added the prefix 'Fantasie' to Chopin's original title 'Impromptu'. The work was first played by Marcellina Czartoryska in Paris, March 1855.

MS. A copy by Marcellina Czartoryska, entitled 'Impromptu inédit Par Frédéric Chopin': Arthur Hedley, London.

88

ANDANTE SPIANATO in G major, for PF. Solo, Op. 22. 1834

For details of the publication of Op. 22, see 58.

This work, although for PF. Solo, was composed as an introduction for the Polonaise in E flat major when this was published as Op. 22. The whole work appeared as *Grande Polonaise Brillante précédée d'un Andante Spianato.*

Wessel published the work as Book XXXIV of the 'Album des Pianistes de Première Force.' The French edition gives the English publishers, erroneously, as Mori & Lavenu (see 58).

MS. State Collection, Warsaw. It is inscribed to Maria Wodzińska with whom, in the autumn of 1835, Chopin had become reacquainted.

89

FOUR MAZURKAS, Op. 24. 1834–1835

No. 1 in G minor.
No. 2 in C major.
No. 3 in A flat major.
No. 4 in B flat minor.

Publication:

Breitkopf & Haertel, Leipzig (5647). January 1836.
M. Schlesinger, Paris (1870). January 1836.
Wessel, London (1645). May 1836.

Dedicated to M. le Comte de Perthuis, an aide-de-camp of Louis-Phillippe, officier d'ordnance.

No. 3, in A flat, may possibly have been sketched in Warsaw before 1831. See MS. (2) below.

Wessel re-issued the work as no. 80 in his series 'L'amateur Pianiste'.

The French edition was announced in November 1835, but not published until two months later.

MSS. (1) The whole opus: Chopin Institute, Warsaw.
    (2) No. 3, in A flat, inscribed by Chopin 'à Mme. Linde' (see 10), and dated '22 September 1835, Dresden': Society of Music, Warsaw.

90

Two Polonaises, Op. 26. 1834–1835

No. 1 in C sharp minor.
No. 2 in E flat minor.

Publication:

Breitkopf & Haertel, Leipzig (5707). July 1836.
M. Schlesinger, Paris (1929). July 1836.
Wessel, London (1647). October 1836.

Dedicated to Josef Dessauer (1798–1876), born in Prague,

and an ardent, not untalented, amateur composer. He lived in Paris from 1833–1834, and again from 1840–1842. Dessauer was a friend of George Sand, who portrayed him in her play *Maitre Favilla*.

Schlesinger's edition was published as a supplement for subscribers to his journal *Gazette Musicale*, 31 July 1836.

The English edition was entitled *Les Favourites*. Wessel re-issued the work as no. 83 in his series 'L'amateur Pianiste'.

Some editions, e.g. Jurgenson's, edited by Karl Klindworth, and Wessel's, omit the vital *da capo* from the end of the first polonaise, in C sharp minor.

MS. Lost.

91

NOCTURNE in C sharp minor, Op. 27: no. 1. 1835

Publication:

    Breitkopf & Haertel, Leipzig (5666). May 1836.

    M. Schlesinger, Paris (1935). July 1836.

    Wessel, London (1648). November 1836.

Op. 27 was dedicated to Mme. la Comtesse d'Apponyi, wife of the Austrian Ambassador to France. Comtesse d'Apponyi, *née* Therese Nogarola—the 'divine Therese', was frequently hostess to Chopin.

For Op. 27: no. 2, see 96.

Schlesinger's edition had been advertised the previous December.

The English edition of the opus was entitled *Les Plaintives*. Wessel re-issued it later as no. 84 in his series 'L'amateur Pianiste'.

MS. Together with Op. 27: no. 2: Schott's Sons, Mainz.

92

WALTZ in G flat major, Op. 70: no. 1 (Posth.). (?) 1835

For details of the publication of Op. 70, see 40.

The date of composition is as given by Fontana, but it is doubtful. There were sketches for the Waltz, almost indecipherable, among the papers of the Chopin family *c*. 1855, and these must date from before 1831.

MS. Lost.

93

TWO MAZURKAS, Op. 67 (Posth.). 1835

    No. 1 in G major.
    No. 3 in C major.

Publication of Op. 67:
    A. M. Schlesinger, Berlin (4393). May 1855.
    J. Meissonnier fils, Paris (3524). February 1856.

Meissonnier's editions of the posthumous works were published without opus numbers.

No. 1, in G major, was written for Mlle. Mlokosiewicz. See Chopin's letter to Fontana of 7 October 1841.

No. 3, in C major, was written for Mme. Hoffmann. Mme. Klementyna Hoffmann, *née* Tańska, an authoress, was the wife of the French author Charles A. Hoffmann.

For Op. 67: no. 2, see **167**; for Op. 67: no. 4, see **163**.

MS. Lost.

94

WALTZ in A flat major, Op. 34: no. 1. Tetschen, 15 September 1835

Publication:

Breitkopf & Haertel, Leipzig (6032). December 1838.
M. Schlesinger, Paris (2715). December 1838.
Wessel, London (2280). December 1838.

Dedicated to Mlle. de Thun-Hohenstein, daughter of a wealthy and cultured family at Tetschen (Czech: Děčín), friends of the composer. Tetschen is a town on the way from Prague to Dresden, in Bohemia, where Chopin stayed with the Thun-Hohenstein family during September 1835.

For Op. 34: no. 2 and Op. 34: no. 3, see **64** and **118** respectively.

MS. (1) Inscribed 'à Mlle. J. de Thun-Hohenstein': in an album in the possesssion of the Thun family. This version differs from the published one.

(2) A second autograph, originally with Breitkopf & Haertel: unknown.

95

WALTZ in A flat major, Op. 69: no. 1 (Posth.) ('L'Adieu' Waltz). Dresden, 24 September 1835

\# This note is dotted in M S (1)
\#\# d♭ in M S (1)
† c in M S (1)

Publication:

    A. M. Schlesinger, Berlin (4395). May 1855.

    J. Meissonnier fils, Paris (3526). February 1856.

    See also note to the dedication below, and note to MS. (3).

Meissonnier's editions of the posthumous works were published without opus numbers.

Dedicated to Maria Wodzińska (1819–1896), who was a sister of boyhood friends of Chopin (Anton, Casimir and Feliks). She and the composer became re-acquainted in September 1835 and he fell in love with her. A member of her family, Count Wodziński, wrote the biographical novel *Trois Romans de Frédéric Chopin*, Paris, 1886, in which the Waltz is, for the first time, reproduced in facsimile. The composer has written on the autograph 'pour Mlle. Marie' and added the date and place. Maria entitled her copy 'L'Adieu' (see below).

A copy in the Chopin family papers appears in Louise's list, dated by her '1836'.

The Waltz is often wrongly designated in trade catalogues and concert programmes as being in F minor.

For Op. 69: no. 2, the Waltz in B minor, see **35**.

MSS. (1) Maria's copy: State Collection, Warsaw.

(2) Copy inscribed by the composer 'à Mme. Peruzzi: hommage de F. F. Chopin, 1838': Harvard University, Dumbarton Oaks, U.S.A. Mme. Peruzzi was the wife of the ambassador of the Duke of Tuscany to the French court.

(3) Copy inscribed by the composer 'à Mlle. Charlotte de Rothschild: hommage de F. F. Chopin, Paris, 1842': Conservatoire, Paris. There are variants in this copy. It was reproduced in facsimile in the periodical *Peuple Amis*, Paris, 1949, page 55, and was first published in the *Oxford Edition of Chopin's Works*, London, 1932 (vol. I).

(4) Copy made by Auguste Franchomme for Jane Stirling, on 22 May 1850: Jagielloński Library, Cracow University. There are further variants in this copy.

96

NOCTURNE in D flat major, Op. 27: no. 2. Autumn 1835

For details of the publication of Op. 27, see 91.

Mendelssohn wrote to his family from Leipzig on 6 October 1835: 'He [Chopin] has such a pretty new nocturne'.

MSS. (1) Chopin Institute, Warsaw. (This manuscript, originally with Breitkopf & Haertel, carries an indication '8ᵉ Nocturne' crossed through by the composer. It was, in fact, the eighth nocturne to be published.)

(2) Schott's Sons, Mainz (see 91).

97

STUDY in F minor, Op. 25: no. 2. January 1836

For details of the publication of Op. 25, see **78**.

MSS. (1) First sketch, dated '27 January 1836': Arthur Hedley, London. This marked *Presto Agitato*.

    (2) Fair copy, written at Dresden and dated '1836', with the indication *agitato*: State Collection, Warsaw (together with Op. 25: no. 1).

    (3) Fair copy, together with Op. 25: no. 1: Chopin Institute, Warsaw. This manuscript, originally with Breitkopf & Haertel, is headed 'pour être publier 15 Octobre.'

98

STUDY in C sharp minor, Op. 25: no. 7. Early 1836

For details of the publication of Op. 25, see **78**.

MS. Unknown, formerly with Edouard Frank.

99

Two Studies, from Op. 25. 1836

No. 3 in F major.
No. 12 in C minor.

For details of the publication of Op. 25, see **78**.

Schumann refers to No. 12, in C minor, as 'a late one'.

MS. No. 3, in F major: unknown, formerly with Edouard
Frank.

100

Two Preludes, from Op. 28. 1836

No. 7 in A major.
No. 17 in A flat major.

No.17 Allegretto

For details of the publication of Op. 28, see **107**.

The date of the A major Prelude is known from the fact that Chopin wrote it in Delphine Potocka's Album in 1836. The A flat Prelude is also of this period. In his note of 1837 to Fontana, Chopin wrote: '. . . copy out for me the A flat Prelude; I want to give it to Perthuis' (see **89**).

MSS. (1) No. 7, in A major: Delphine Potocka's Album (see **35**).

(2) The same: Chopin Institute, Warsaw, in a manuscript containing all the Preludes.

(3) No. 17, in A flat major: Gesellschaft der Musikfreunde, Vienna. This belonged to Clara Schumann. She bequeathed it to Brahms, from whom it passed to its present owners. M. Alfred Cortot considers this MS. not to be in Chopin's hand, in which case it may be the copy, referred to above, made by Fontana.

(4) The same: Chopin Institute, Warsaw, in a manuscript containing all the Preludes.

(5) The same. Eight bars, inscribed 'Paris, 9 November 1839 de la part de l'ami F. F. Chopin', written in the album of Ignaz Moscheles: Sotheby, London, 8 December, 1959.

101

SONG for voice and PF., Op. 74: no. 17. 1836

'Śpiew grobowy' ('Leci liscie z drzewa')
'Hymn from the Tomb' ('The leaves drift from the trees').

(E flat minor)

German title: 'Polens Grabgesang'. English title: 'Poland's Dirge'.

Text: Wincenty Pol.

For details of the publication of Op. 74, see 32.

The 'Hymn from the Tomb' was published later than the rest of Op. 74, *c.* 1872, by Schlesinger of Berlin. (1872: incorporated with the other sixteen songs of Op. 74; 1873: as a separate song.) Fontana's intention was to include only sixteen songs in Op. 74, since, as he recalled in his letter of 1853 to Chopin's sister, Louise, the composer had had a superstitious dread of the number '7'.

An arrangement of the song for PF. Solo, called 'Chant de Tombeau', made by Rudolf Hasolf, appeared from Schlesinger in 1861 (P.N. 5139) and was called 'Op. 75'. At the same time a PF. Duet arrangement (P.N. 5140) was also published. These PF. arrangements preceded the publication of the song itself. The English edition of Stanley Lucas & Weber (1874) gives this 'Hymn from the Tomb', but in Peters's edition (1887) it is omitted.

It has been stated, but without any documentary evidence, that the song was composed by Chopin actually on 3 May 1836—the 'Third of May' which commemorates the founding of Poland's constitution.

MS. Lost.

A copy used by Schlesinger is in the possession of Antony van Hoboken, Ascona; it is not in Fontana's hand. He had no copy, in fact, in 1855 during his preparations for Op. 74.[1]

[1] See the *Musical Quarterly*, New York, January 1956.

BALLADE no. 2, in F major, Op. 38. First version: 1836; final version: Majorca, January 1839

Publication:

Breitkopf & Haertel, Leipzig (6330). October 1840.
Troupenas, Paris (925). September 1840.
Wessel, London (3555). October 1840.

Dedicated to Schumann.

The work is said to be based on ideas from the poem 'Świteź', by Adam Mickiewicz.

The composer rarely played the whole Ballade; this may account for Schumann's remarks that when he heard the composer play it at Leipzig in 1836 the middle section (*presto con fuoco*) and the coda (*agitato*) were missing and therefore composed later.

The English edition is entitled *La Gracieuse*.

Chopin wrote to Fontana in April 1840: 'Troupenas has bought my seven compositions and will do business with Wessel direct.' This Ballade is the earliest of the seven works to which the composer refers; the others are:

(*a*) SONATA in B flat minor, Op. 35,
(*b*) IMPROMPTU in F sharp minor, Op. 36,
(*c*) Two NOCTURNES, G minor and G major, Op. 37,
(*d*) SCHERZO in C sharp minor, Op. 39,
(*e*) Two POLONAISES, A major and C minor, Op. 40,
(*f*) FOUR MAZURKAS, E minor, C sharp minor, B major and A flat major, Op. 41.

MSS. (1) Rudolf Nydahl, Stockholm (formerly with Ernst Rudorff, and Peters's Musikbibliothek, Leipzig).

(2) Bibliothèque du Conservatoire de Musique, Paris. At the end of this MS., page 9, in another hand, are the words: 'À mon cher Ch. Ritter. P. Seligmann bien heureux de lui offrir ce MS. de F. Chopin.'

103

SONG for voice and PF., Op. 74: no. 14. Dresden, 8 September 1836

'Pierścień' ('Smutno niańki, ci śpiewały')
'The Ring' ('I am sad, nurse').

(E flat major)

German title: 'Das Ringlein'.
Text: Stefan Witwicki.

For details of the publication of Op. 74, see 32.

The four-bar prelude given in some editions is not authentic. Liszt transcribed the song for PF. Solo, published by Schlesinger, 1860 (see 32).

MSS. (1) State Collection, Warsaw. It is inscribed 'Drezno, 8 7bre 1836'.

(2) Another copy, previously owned by Fontana: on sale in Paris, November, 1959.

104

STUDY in A flat major, Op. 25: no. 1. Dresden, early September 1836

For details of the publication of Op. 25, see **78**.

This is the 'Shepherd Boy' Study.

An autograph copy of the Study was sent to Clara Wieck accompanied by a note from the composer: 'à Mlle. Clara Wieck par son admirateur. Leipzig, 12 September 1836.' This note was kept by a later owner together with a MS. of the Polonaise in A flat, Op. 53. This fortuitous association led to the supposition that Chopin was offering the Polonaise to Mlle. Wieck. The erroneous conclusion was then drawn that the A flat Polonaise had been written, or at least sketched, as early as 1836.

MSS. (1) Fair copy (together with Op. 25: no. 1, in F minor): State Collection, Warsaw. This copy is headed 'Dresden, 1836'.

     (2) Fair copy (together with the F minor Study): Chopin Institute, Warsaw (see **97**).

105

FOUR MAZURKAS, Op. 30. 1836–1837

    No. 1 in C minor.
    No. 2 in B minor.
    No. 3 in D flat major.
    No. 4 in C sharp minor.

Publication:

> Breitkopf & Haertel, Leipzig (5851). January 1838.
> M. Schlesinger, Paris (2489). January 1838.
> Wessel, London (2170). December 1837.

Dedicated to Mme. la Princesse de Württemberg (*née* Czartoryska).

No. 4, in C sharp minor, was sketched earlier than 1836.

The opus was presented to readers of the Paris *Gazette Musicale* as a supplement on 25 March 1838.

MS. Chopin Institute, Warsaw. (A copy in another hand).

106

Two Nocturnes, Op. 32. 1836–1837

> No. 1 in B major.
> No. 2 in A flat major.

Publication:

A. M. Schlesinger, Berlin (2180). December 1837.
M. Schlesinger, Paris (2500). December 1837.
Wessel, London (2169). December 1837.

Dedicated to Mme. la Baronne de Billing, *née* Camille de Courbonne, a pupil of Chopin and on intimate terms with him, enough to call him in a letter a 'charmant sylph'.

A. M. Schlesinger included the second Nocturne in an *Album des Pianistes*, No. 2. This was 'A Collection inédites, modernes et brillantes', published in late 1837, although dated '1838'.

The English edition was entitled *Il lamento e la consolazione*. MS. Lost.

107

Seventeen Preludes, from Op. 28. 1836 to November 1838

No. 3 in G major.	No. 15 in D flat major.
No. 5 in D major.	No. 16 in B flat minor.
No. 6 in B minor.	No. 18 in F minor.
No. 8 in F sharp minor.	No. 19 in E flat major.
No. 9 in E major.	No. 20 in C minor.
No. 11 in B major.	No. 22 in G minor.
No. 12 in G sharp minor.	No. 23 in F major.
No. 13 in F sharp major.	No. 24 in D minor.
No. 14 in E flat minor.	

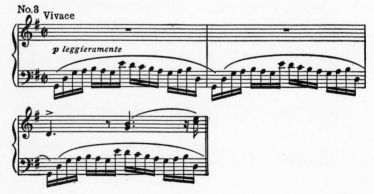

Publication:

> Breitkopf & Haertel, Leipzig (6088). September 1839.
> Adolphe Catelin, Paris (560). June 1839.
> Wessel, London (Book I, 3098; Book II, 3099). January 1840.

The French and English editions were dedicated to Camille Pleyel (1788–1855), pianist, composer, publisher and PF. manufacturer.

The German edition was dedicated to Joseph Christoph Kessler (1800–1872), Bohemian pianist and composer, an acquaintance of Count Potocki. Kessler's twenty-four Preludes, Op. 31, had been dedicated to Chopin.

The French edition, published in two parts, carried no opus number; this is because Chopin in a letter to his publisher written from Marseilles on 17 March 1839, was unable to recall it. The absence of an opus number on these Preludes persisted in France for long after Chopin's death (*c.* 1860). Schlesinger's successor in the Paris business, Brandus, purchased the copyright of the Preludes from Catelin *c.* 1844.

The English edition likewise carried no opus number and was also published in two parts, Wessel entitling them the 5th and 6th books of *Studies*. He announced the publication of them as early as October 1839. Later, apparently, '28' was added to the blank 'Op.', but on Book II only.

The reservation of the number '28' for these preludes on publication (by June 1839 the composer's opus numbers had reached 34) suggests that the idea of publishing a collection of preludes had been in Chopin's mind from the time that Op. 27 had been published, at the end of 1835, and that in all probability the composition of some of them had been begun by then.

(*a*) No. 8, in F sharp minor, was believed by Liszt to be the Prelude inspired by the rainstorm at Valdemosa (see (*d*) below).

(*b*) No. 9, in E major, was transcribed by Liszt for Organ Solo, published by Schuberth, Leipzig, in Gottschalg's *Repertorium für Orgel*, no. 8, *c*. 1864.

(*c*) No. 14, in E flat minor, carries in most editions the direction *Allegro*. Edouard Ganche in his *Oxford Edition* of the composer's works (London, 1932) states that in Jane Stirling's copy of the Prelude (the French Edition) Chopin himself emended the word to *Largo*.

(*d*) No. 15, in D flat major, is the 'Raindrop' Prelude. Both it and No. 6, in B minor, have been claimed as the music which George Sand mentioned in her description of the rainstorm at Valdemosa.[1]

(*e*) No. 20, in C minor: the disputed note in the last chord of bar 3, given in most editions as E♮, is stated by Ganche (*loc. cit.*) to be E♭, since Chopin had pencilled in a flat before the printed E in Jane Stirling's copy.

See also **100, 123, 124.** For the Prelude in A flat, see **86**; for the Prelude in C sharp minor, see **141**.

MSS. The complete set of Preludes: Chopin Institute, Warsaw. The manuscript, Chopin's fair copy made from existing sketches and fair copies, shows many alterations. These may be due to last minute revisions, or to mistakes of copying afterwards corrected. It bears a dedication in Chopin's hand to J. C. Kessler,

---

[1] See *Musical Times*, London, August 1957.

but the manuscript went to Catelin, Paris and not to Breitkopf & Haertel. The German publishers received Fontana's copy of the Preludes. This copy of Fontana's, frequently mistaken for an autograph copy by Chopin, is in private possession.

108

NOCTURNE in C minor. 1837

Publication:

> *Towartzystwo Wydawnicze Muzyki Polskiego* ('Society for the Publication of Polish Music'), no. 83, Warsaw, Spring 1938. Edited by Ludwig Brońarski, together with the Largo in E flat (**109**).

Attention was first drawn to this unpublished work, and to the Largo in E flat, by an article in the *Polski Rocznik Muzykologiczny* ('Polish Musicological Annual'), Warsaw, 1937.

The piece, forty-five bars long, may be a rejected item from Op. 32 (**106**). It was later republished by Alfred Cortot in 'L'Edition de travail des *Oeuvres Posthumes* de Chopin'.

MSS. (1) Sketch of the opening bars, differing from the final version.

(2) Final version, fair copy.

Both in the Conservatoire, Paris.

109

LARGO in E flat major. (?) 1837

Publication:

> *Towartzystwo Wydawnicze Muzyki Polskiego*, no. 83,
> Warsaw, Spring 1938 (see previous item).

The manuscript of the work, sixteen bars long, is simply
dated '6 July' and the year of composition is unknown. If
its association in the Paris Conservatoire Library with the
previous item gives any grounds for believing that it is of
the same period, then the work may be a rejected prelude.
Its style faintly resembles that of the C minor Prelude,
Op. 28: no. 20.

MS. Conservatoire, Paris.

110

IMPROMPTU no. 1, in A flat major, Op. 29. 1837

Publication:

> Breitkopf & Haertel, Leipzig (5850). January 1838.
> M. Schlesinger, Paris (2467). October 1837.
> Wessel, London (2166). October 1837.

Dedicated to Mlle. la Comtesse Caroline de Lobau.
The English edition was called 'Op. 28' for many years.

It was advertised, as on sale, in the *Musical World*, 20 October 1837.

Schlesinger's edition was published as a Supplement for subscribers to his journal *Gazette Musicale*, 29 October 1837.

MS. Deutsche Staatsbibliothek, Berlin (now in the State Collection, Warsaw).

III

SCHERZO no. 2, in B flat minor, Op. 31. 1837

Publication:

> Breitkopf & Haertel, Leipzig (5852). February 1838.
> M. Schlesinger, Paris (2494). December 1837.
> Wessel, London (2168). December 1837.

Dedicated to Mlle. la Comtesse Adèle de Fürstenstein.
Wessel entitled his edition *Le Méditation*.

MSS. (1) Chopin Institute, Warsaw. (A copy in another hand).
(2) Conservatoire, Paris (given after Chopin's death by his sister Louise to Thomas Tellefsen).

112

SONG for voice and PF., Op. 74: no. 12. 1837

> 'Moja pieszczotka' ('Moja pieszczotka gdy wesołej').
> 'My Darling' ('My darling when you are happily singing').

(G flat major)

German title: 'Meine Freuden'.
Text: Adam Mickiewicz.

For details of the publication of Op. 74, see **32**.

Liszt transcribed this song for PF. Solo, see **32**.

MS. Sketch, in A flat major: Cracow Music Society. On the
     manuscript Chopin has written 'w Ges trzeba śpiewac'
     ('transpose into G flat'). The successive owners of this
     MS. have written their names on it: T. Kwiatowski,
     1872; Marcelline Czartoryska; Stanisłav Tarnowski,
     26 February 1885. There is a facsimile of the MS. in
     Binental's *Documents and Souvenirs of Chopin*, Warsaw,
     1930.

113

VARIATION no. 6, in E major (Largo), for the *Hexameron*.
1837

Publication:

> Tobias Haslinger, Vienna (7700). 1839.
> Bernard Latte, Paris (. . .). 1839.
> Cramer & Co., London (406). 1839.

Dedicated to Mme. la Princesse Christine de Belgiojoso.

The *Hexameron* was a collection of six variations for PF.
Solo on the March in Bellini's opera *I Puritani di Scozia*

contributed by Liszt, Thalberg, Pixis, Herz, Czerny and Chopin. The Introduction, Theme, bridge passages and Finale were composed by Liszt, who also arranged a shortened version for two pianofortes published by Schuberth, Leipzig, in 1870. (The version for PF. & Orchestra is not by Liszt.) The variations were published as: *Hexameron*, Morceau de Concert. Grandes Variations de Bravoura pour Piano sur le Marche des Puritans de Bellini.' It was composed for Princess Christine de Belgiojoso, who wished to raise money from its sales for impoverished exiles. It was first performed in 1837 (a date wrongly given on occasions as the date of publication.)

The Vienna edition gives Mori, London, as the English publisher; this is an error.

Vincenzio Bellini (1801–1835): the first performance of *I Puritani* took place in the Théâtre-Italien, Paris, on 25 January 1835.

MS. Lost.

114

FUNERAL MARCH from the Sonata no. 1, in B flat minor, Op. 35. 1837

For details of the publication of Op. 35, see **128**.

The movement was composed first, but only published with the complete sonata. Following the news of Chopin's death, Wessel, London, Troupenas, Paris and Breitkopf & Haertel, Leipzig, simultaneously published the March as an independent composition on 17 November 1849.

MS. The complete Sonata: Chopin Institute, Warsaw (this MS. is possibly Fontana's copy).

115

FOUR MAZURKAS, Op. 33. 1837–1838

 No. 1 in G sharp minor.
 No. 2 in D major.
 No. 3 in C major.
 No. 4 in B minor.

Publication:

 Breitkopf & Haertel, Leipzig (5985). November 1838.
 M. Schlesinger, Paris (2714). October 1838.
 Wessel, London (2279). November 1838.

Dedicated to Mlle. la Comtesse Rosa Mostowska, daughter of the Minister of Public Information.

The original tempo on the composer's MS. of No. 1, in G sharp minor, is *Presto*. He seems, according to one or two copies in the possession of pupils of his, to have changed the tempo later to *Lento*.

No. 3, in C major, is the mazurka which is supposed to have led to a quarrel between Chopin and Meyerbeer over the time-signature.

Schlesinger published these mazurkas as a supplement to his journal *Gazette Musicale*, 28 October 1838. In this supplement the C major and D major Mazurkas were Nos. 2 and 3 respectively.

Two of the mazurkas were republished by Breitkopf & Haertel in a collection called *Album für PF. & Gesänge für 1839*.

MSS. (1) Fragments of No. 1 and No. 4, with the title page: Chopin Institute, Warsaw.

(2) Fair copy of No. 1: unknown. There is a facsimile of the greater part of this copy in Adolf Weissmann's *Chopin*, Berlin, 1912. In this autograph there are only four sharps in the key-signature and it is printed thus in Breitkopf's edition above.

(3) Fair copy of No. 2: unknown. The greater part of this copy (bars 1–30) was reproduced in the 'Mazurkas' volume of the Breitkopf & Haertel edition of Chopin's works, edited by Ignaz Friedmann, 1929.

(4) Fair copy of No. 3 (headed by Chopin 'No. 2'): unknown. The MSS. (2) (3) and (4) were sold by Leo Liepmannssohn, Berlin, in May 1930.

(5) No. 4: Library of Congress, Washington, D.C., U.S.A. (This may be a copy in the hand of Fontana.)

116

SONG for voice and PF., Op. 74: no. 2. 1838

'Wiosna' ('Błyszczą krople rosy mruczy zdrój po błoni') 'Spring' ('The dew glistens, the stream gushes through the fields').

(G minor)

German Title: 'Frühling'.
Text: Stefan Witwicki.

For details of the publication of Op. 74, see **32**.

Liszt transcribed the song for PF. Solo (*6 Chants Polonais*, no. 2), published by A. M. Schlesinger, Berlin, 1860. For Chopin's own arrangement for PF. Solo, see next.

MSS. (1) Baron L. Kronenburg, Warsaw.

      (2) The voice part, with words added, and dated '1 September 1848', written in the Album of Miss Fanny Erskine: Fitzwilliam Museum, Cambridge. (Miss Erskine was a niece of Jane Stirling.)

117

ANDANTINO in G minor; an arrangement for PF. Solo of the song 'Wiosna' ('Spring'), Op. 74: no. 2. Five manuscripts: April 1838 to 1 September 1848.

Unpublished

MSS. (1) This version, the earliest, is dated April 1838: unknown.

      (2) A second version, written on both sides of an album leaf, with mauve borders, inscribed at the end 'á Madame Kiéré, hommage respecteux de son devoué Chopin': Sotheby, London, 17 June 1958. Mme. Kiéré was a Parisian hostess, and a friend of Fanny Herschel, sister of Mendelssohn.

(3) A third version, signed by the composer, and dated 'Paris, 5 February 1846': Gesellschaft der Musikfreunde, Vienna (presented by Count Victor Wimpffen, in 1898). The title *Andantino* and ' "Wiosna": Paroles de Witwicki' have been added by another hand. There is a reproduction in *Chopin und Wien*, Franz Zagiba, Vienna, 1951.

(4) A fourth version, dated 'London, 28 June 1848', extremely minute in size: Album of Mrs. S. Horsley, London.

(5) A fifth version, dated 'Manchester, 1 September 1848': unknown. See also **116**.

118

WALTZ in F major, Op. 34: no. 3. 1838

Publication:

Breitkopf & Haertel, Leipzig (6034). December 1838.
M. Schlesinger, Paris (2717). December 1838.
Wessel, London (2282). December 1838.

Dedicated to Mlle. A. d'Eichtal, daughter of Baron d'Eichtal, and a pupil of Chopin. At the house of Baron d'Eichtal Charles Hallé first heard Chopin play. The composer wrote in his letter of August 1839 to Fontana: '. . . tell me whether you took a waltz from me to Mlle. Eichtal.'

The three waltzes of Op. 34 were included by Schlesinger in an *Album des Pianistes* announced on 15 November 1838 in the *Gazette Musicale* as consisting of new and unpublished pieces (with portraits of the composers) by Thalberg,

Chopin, Doehler, Liszt, Osborne and Mèreaux. Amedée Mèreaux's contribution was a 'Fantasia on a Mazurka by Chopin'.

Chopin was annoyed by the inclusion of his waltzes in this *Album*: see his letter to Fontana of 28 December 1838.

This Waltz in F major is the so-called 'Cat' Waltz. For Op. 34: no. 1, see **94**; for Op. 34: no. 2, see **64**.

MS. Lost.

119

NOCTURNE in G minor, Op. 37: no. 1. 1838

Publication:

> Breitkopf & Haertel, Leipzig (6334). June 1840.
> Troupenas, Paris (893). June 1840.
> Wessel, London (3554). July 1840.

There is no dedication of Op. 37. For the Nocturne in G major, Op. 37: no. 2, see **127**.

The English edition is entitled *Les Soupirs*.

MS. Chopin Institute, Warsaw, together with **127**. This manuscript, originally with Breitkopf & Haertel, is not an autograph, although possibly corrected in Chopin's hand.

120

POLONAISE in A major, Op. 40: no. 1. October 1838

Publication:

> Breitkopf & Haertel, Leipzig (6331). December 1840.
> Troupenas, Paris (977). December 1840.
> Wessel, London (3557). November 1841.

Dedicated to Julian Fontana (1810–1869), a friend and fellow-pupil of Chopin's at the Warsaw Conservatoire. After 1830 he, like Chopin, settled in Paris.

He asked Chopin to alter the middle section of this Polonaise, and the composer replied: 'I will alter the second half of the Polonaise for you until I die.' It had been Chopin's intention to dedicate this Polonaise to Titus Woyciechowski, and its companion, Op. 40: no. 2, in C minor, to Fontana. The inscription on the autograph copy runs: '2 Polonaises dediés à T.W. / son ami Julius Fontana', but on publication the 'T.W.' was omitted (MS. (2) below).

For Op. 40: no. 2, see next.

Wessel called the Polonaises of Op. 40 *Les Favourites*, as well as those of Op. 26.

MSS. (1) British Museum (together with Op. 40: no. 2). These autographs were the basis of Troupenas' edition.[1]

(2) (Thaddeus Jentysie): the autograph was found in his posthumous papers, its present whereabouts unknown. The first page was reproduced in facsimile by the *Echo Muzyczne*, Warsaw, October 1899, the fiftieth anniversary of Chopin's death. The whole MS. was reproduced in Binental's *Chopin: Life and Art*, Warsaw, 1937.

(3) Chopin Institute, Warsaw (together with Op. 40: no. 2). (A copy in another hand).

---

[1] It was Chopin's practice, to save the bother of writing out repeats, to letter the bars alphabetically and then leave a corresponding number of blank bars, each bearing its appropriate letter. In this MS. the 15th bar of the 'Trio' section bears the letter 'p' (Chopin omitted 'k'). This was misinterpreted in Troupenas' edition as 'piano', and reproduced thus in subsequent editions. The fact was first pointed out by Dr. Oswald Jonas, Chicago.

121

POLONAISE in C minor, Op. 40: no. 2. Sketched October 1838, finished Majorca, early 1839

For details of the publication of Op. 40, see previous item.

The opening theme has been compared to that of Kurpinski's 'Coronation' Polonaise, set to the words 'Hail! O King!', and written for Alexander I, 1825. Chopin's theme is claimed to be a minor-key variant:

MSS. (1) British Museum, together with Op. 40: no. 1.
        (2) Chopin Institute, Warsaw, together with Op. 40: no. 1. (A copy in another hand).

122

MAZURKA in E minor, Op. 41: no. 2. Majorca, 28 November 1838

Publication of Op. 41:

Breitkopf & Haertel, Leipzig (6335). December 1840.
Troupenas, Paris (978). December 1840.
Wessel, London (3558). May 1841.

For the other three mazurkas of Op. 41, see **126**.

Dedicated to Étienne (=Stefan) Witwicki.

MSS. (1) Gregor Piatigorsky, Los Angeles (former owners:
Pauline Viardot-Garcia and Henry Fatio). The
MS. is headed 'Palma. 28 9br'. At the foot of the
first page of the MS. is a sketch of the Prelude in
E minor, Op. 28: no. 4. On the next page are
sketches for the Prelude in A minor, Op. 28: no.
2, and for two other Preludes, afterwards rejected,
in B flat major and C sharp minor. (L. Broñarski:
Music Manuscripts of Chopin at Geneva, Cracow,
1930.)

(2) Incomplete version: Conservatoire, Paris.

(3) Chopin Institute, Warsaw (formerly with Breitkopf & Haertel). (A copy in another hand).

(4) Gesellschaft der Musikfreunde, Vienna. This is
possibly not an autograph, but may be Fontana's
copy. It is, however, signed by Chopin, but not
dated by him.

123

FOUR PRELUDES from Op. 28. Palma, Majorca, November
to December 1838

No. 2 in A minor.
No. 4 in E minor.
No. 10 in C sharp minor.
No. 21 in B flat major.

For details of the publication of Op. 28, see **107**.

Liszt transcribed No. 4, in E minor, for Organ Solo.

MSS. Sketches of Nos. 2 and 4, see previous item. For the
inclusion of Nos. 10 and 21, see also previous item.
All the preludes: Chopin Institute, Warsaw.

124

PRELUDE in C major, Op. 28: no. 1. (?) Majorca, January
1839

For details of the publication of Op. 28, see **107**.

There is a tradition that this was the last prelude to be composed.

MS. All the preludes: Chopin Institute, Warsaw.

125

SCHERZO no. 3, in C sharp minor, Op. 39. Begun at Majorca, January 1839, finished mid-1839

Publication:

    Breitkopf & Haertel, Leipzig (6332). November 1840.
    Troupenas, Paris (926). December 1840.
    Wessel, London (3556). October 1840.

Dedicated to Adolf Gutman (1819–1882), German pianist and composer, pupil of Chopin.

The work is referred to by Chopin in his letter to Fontana of 17 March 1839 as still unfinished; it was played to Moscheles in the autumn of that year by Gutman.

MS. Chopin Institute, Warsaw. The MS., originally with Breitkopf & Haertel, is inscribed by the composer to 'Gustman'.

126

THREE MAZURKAS from Op. 41. July 1839

    No. 1 in C sharp minor.
    No. 3 in B major.
    No. 4 in A flat major.

For details of the publication of Op. 41, and for Mazurka No. 2, in E minor, see **122**.

The order of the mazurkas in the opus is not standardised. In the thematic catalogue devised for Jane Stirling by Chopin and Franchomme, the order is 1. E minor, 2. B major, 3. A flat major, 4. C sharp minor; this may well be the order of composition. See Chopin's letter to Fontana of August 1839.[1]

MS. All four mazurkas: Chopin Institute, Warsaw. This is the manuscript used by Breitkopf & Haertel having the mazurkas in the order: 1. A flat major, 2. C sharp minor, 3. E minor, 4. B major.

127

NOCTURNE in G major, Op. 37: no. 2. July 1839

---

[1] In this letter, the original of which is owned by Arthur Hedley, Chopin writes quite distinctly of the first mazurka as being in C (*sic*) minor. This may, of course, be a slip of the pen.

For details of the publication of Op. 37, see **119**.
MS. Chopin Institute, Warsaw, together with Op. 37: no. 1.

128

SONATA no. 1, in B flat minor, Op. 35 (first movement, Scherzo and Finale). Summer 1839

Publication:

 Breitkopf & Haertel, Leipzig (6329). May 1840.
 Troupenas, Paris (891). May 1840.
 Wessel, London (3549). July 1840.

There is no dedication of Op. 35.
The slow movement ('Funeral March') had been composed in 1837, see **114**.
A copy of the French edition, inscribed by Chopin to Jane Stirling, is in the Jagielloński Library, Cracow University.
The Sonata was edited by Brahms for the *Gesamtausgabe* of Breitkopf & Haertel (vol. VIII, 1878).

MS. Chopin Institute, Warsaw. This manuscript, originally with Breitkopf & Haertel, is a copy in another hand.

129

IMPROMPTU no. 2, in F sharp major, Op. 36. Early autumn 1839

Publication:

> Breitkopf & Haertel, Leipzig (6333). May 1840.
> Troupenas, Paris (892). May 1840.
> Wessel, London (3550). July 1840.

There is no dedication of Op. 36.

Wessel was prevented by Chopin himself from entitling the work 'Agréements au Salon'.

MSS. (1) Fragmentary sketches: Czartoryski Museum, Cracow. These sketches are bound in with Chopin's manuscript of the 'Krakowiak' Rondo, Op. 14 (see **29**).

(2) Fragment (two pages): Christian Zabriskie, U.S.A.

129 (B)

CANON at the octave in F minor. (?) 1839

Unpublished

The manuscript, a rough draft, consists of nineteen or so bars, with many erasures and corrections.

MS. Nicolas Rauch, Geneva, November 1957.

130

Trois Nouvelles Études. Late autumn 1839

No. 1 in F minor.
No. 2 in A flat major.
No. 3 in D flat major.

Publication:

A. M. Schlesinger, Berlin (2207: 2423). August–September 1840.

M. Schlesinger, Paris (2345). 15 November 1840.

(?) Chappell, London (see below). January 1841.

The three studies were composed at the request of Ignaz Moscheles. They were published in the *Méthode des Méthodes de Moscheles et Fétis*. This was an elaborate pianoforte 'Tutor' in three parts: the first part contained a system of elementary instruction, the second part 'Progressive Exercises', the third part a series of mostly new studies called 'Études de

Perfectionnement', in which these three of Chopin's were included.

In England the work was called *Complete System of Instruction for the Pianoforte* and in Germany *Pianoforte=schule aller Pianoforte=schulen*. The present writer has never seen a copy of Chappell's 'Part III' of this publication, which would contain Chopin's Études. There is a possibility, according to the present proprietors of the firm of Chappell, that 'Part I', not having been a commercial success, was the only part published, and the project abandoned in England. Hence there was no English edition of the *Trois Nouvelles Études* until April 1855, when Jullien & Co., London, published the three studies with an introduction by G. A. MacFarren.

Other contributors to the 'Études de Perfectionnement' were Mendelssohn ('Étude in F minor) and Liszt ('Morceau de Salon').

The first part of the *Méthode* was published in France and Germany in 1837, which accounts for Maurice Schlesinger's Publisher's Number and for the earlier one of A. M. Schlesinger's German edition; the introduction to the whole work, by Fétis, is dated in the French and English editions '1 November 1840'. Chopin's three studies were issued as a separate publication in Paris and Berlin in September, 1841.

A later edition of the first study, in F minor, published by Brandus (successors in the business of M. Schlesinger, Paris) contains variants which almost certainly derive from Chopin himself.

Facsimile of No. 1, in F minor, with a preface by Arthur Hedley: London, 1940.

MSS. (1) No. 1, in F minor, 10 bars, dated '16 January 1841', copied by Chopin into the album of the sculptor Jean Pierre Dantan (1800–1869): Bibliothèque Nationale, Paris.

(2) All three studies: Arthur Hedley, London.

131

WALTZ in A flat major, Op. 42. Spring 1840

Publication:

    Breitkopf & Haertel, Leipzig (6419). July 1840.
    Pacini, Paris (3708). 30 June 1840.
    Wessel, London (3559). July 1840.

There is no dedication of Op. 42.

In his letter of 18 June 1840 to Breitkopf & Haertel, Chopin wrote: 'As Signor Pacini is publishing a waltz of mine in the *Cent-et-un* on the 30th inst., I think it best to send you a proof.'

Cent-et-un was one of Pacini's several 'Albums', that is, serial publications issued approximately twice a month. Each issue contained a collection of works by different composers of the day. *Cent-et-un* consisted of PF. works only; it was announced in February 1838, and was to consist of 25 books, each to contain 10 or 15 pages. Presumably it was to end after the publication of 101 compositions, but the project was never adhered to.

Pacini wrote to Chopin on 22 April 1840 postponing the publication of this waltz, because the next number of *Cent-et-un*, he wrote, would contain works only by Cherubini and Niedermeyer. On 20 June 1840 he wrote asking Chopin for the corrected proofs, one of which, evidently, the composer had forwarded to Breitkopf & Haertel. The Waltz, entitled 'Grande Valse Nouvelle', Op. 42, appeared as 'no. 68 des *Cent-et-un*'.

Pacini's business was purchased by Louël, Paris, *c.* 1850, and from Louël it passed finally to Simon Richault, Paris, in

1866. All Pacini's successors published the waltz with their own imprints.

Wessel entitled the waltz, the *'Cent-et-un* Waltz'! This title was dropped on later issues, however.

The prompt publication of Op. 42 (Op. 41, for instance, composed a year earlier, did not appear until six months after Op. 42) may be due to the different publisher, but is more probably an indication of the popularity of Chopin's waltzes.

MS. Lost.

132

SONG for voice and PF. 25 March 1840

'Dumka' ('Mgła mi do oczu zawiewa złona')
'Dirge' ('Mist before my eyes').

(A minor)

Text: Bohdan Zaleski, from the poem 'Nie ma czego trzeba'. See **156**.

Publication:

The periodical *Słowo Polskie*, Lwow, 22 October 1910, in an issue devoted to the centenary of Chopin's birthyear, edited by Staniław Lam.

Lam discovered the song, which is eight bars long, in 2/4 time, in an Album belonging to Stefan Witwicki. His printed publication was reproduced in facsimile by Maria Mirska in her book *Szlakiem Chopina*, Warsaw, 1935, page **152**.

MS. Lost.

133

WALTZ ('SOSTENUTO') in E flat major. 20 July 1840

Publication:

> Francis, Day & Hunter, London (23100). May 1955.
> (edited by Maurice J. E. Brown.)

The piece, in the nature of a waltz but not so entitled, is 48 bars long and was probably written for Emil Gaillard (see **140**). It was given to the Conservatoire, Paris, by Joseph Gaillard in 1938.

MS. Conservatoire, Paris. It is signed by the composer and dated 'Paris, 20 July 1840'. 1840 is the one year in the decade when Chopin was not at Nohant, the home of George Sand, during the summer months.

134

MAZURKA in A minor (*Notre Temps*). Summer 1840

Publication:

> B. Schott's Sons, Mainz (6493/2). It was No. 2 of the 'Album' entitled 'Notre Temps'. February 1842.
> Republished by:
>> (*a*) Troupenas, Paris (978), as 'Mazurka Élégante', January 1845.
>> (*b*) Wessel, London (6316). January 1846.

Notre Temps was the general title of twelve pieces com-
posed by Czerny, Chopin, Kalliwoda, Rosenheim, Thalberg,
Kalkbrenner, Mendelssohn, Bertini, Wolff, Kontski,
Osborne and Hertz. Mendelssohn's contribution was the
'Prelude and Fugue in E minor'. The 'Album' was on sale
through agents in Leipzig (Breitkopf) and Vienna (H. F.
Müller).

The French republication was advertised in the journal
La France Musicale, 5 January 1845, as on sale at the 'Bureau
Central de Musique'. Troupenas's business was bought *c.*
1850 by Brandus.

Wessel, without authorisation, entitled his edition *The
Cracow Mazurka*, and gave it the opus number 'Op. 59: *bis*'.

MS. Lost.

135

POLONAISE in F sharp minor, Op. 44. Late 1840 to August
1841

Publication:

> Pietro Mechetti, Vienna (3577). November 1841.
> M. Schlesinger, Paris (3477). November 1841.
> Wessel, London (5226) [*sic*]. March 1842.

Dedicated to Mme. la Princesse Charles de Beauvau (*née*
Komar), a sister of Delphine Potocka (see Chopin's letter to
his parents, 21 November 1830).

In his letter to Fontana of 25 August 1841, Chopin wrote,
'. . . a new kind of Polonaise, but it is more a fantasia.'
These words refer to this piece, since two days previously

he had written to Mechetti, offering a 'Fantasia en forme de Polonaise' for 25 Louis d'Or.

Wessel's Publisher's Number is an error for '5296'.

MS. Lost.

136

BALLADE no. 3, in A flat major, Op. 47. Sketched 1840, finished summer 1841

Publication:

Breitkopf & Haertel, Leipzig (6652). January 1842: advertised in December 1841.

M. Schlesinger, Paris (3486). November 1841.

Wessel, London (5299). March 1842.

Dedicated to Mlle. Pauline de Noailles, a favourite pupil of Chopin's.

MS. Chopin Institute, Warsaw.
(The copy in the Conservatoire, Paris, was made by Saint-Saëns.)

137

FANTASIA in F minor, Op. 49. Sketched early 1841, finished May 1841

Publication:

  Breitkopf & Haertel, Leipzig (6654). January 1842.
  M. Schlesinger, Paris (3489). November 1841.
  Wessel, London (5301) [*sic*]. March 1842.

Dedicated to Mme. la Princesse Catherine de Souzzo, a pupil of Chopin's. The composer wrote to his family on 20 July 1845 of her mother, Princess Obreskowa: 'I have had many proofs of her kindheartedness, and am very fond of her. She is very devoted to music.'

For his letter to Breitkopf & Haertel of 4 May 1841 mentioning this work and the 'Allegro de Concert', Op. 46, see **142**.

Wessel's Publisher's Number is an error for '5302'; '5301' is the Nocturne, Op. 48 : no. 2. (**142**).

MS. Chopin Institute, Warsaw.

138

WALTZ in F minor, Op. 70 : no. 2 (Posth.). June 1841

For details of the publication of Op. 70, see **40**.

The Waltz may have been written earlier than 1841: in the list devised by Chopin's sister Louise, it is dated '1840–41'. It was evidently a composition kept by Chopin for private gifts to friends; six, or possibly seven, copies are extant and details are given, in connection with each one, below. Variants are found chiefly in the opening bars of the Waltz as quoted here.

MSS. (1) Inscribed 'à Mlle. Marie de Krudner, Paris, le 8 juin 1841': Conservatoire, Paris.

    (2) Inscribed 'à Mme. Oury, Paris, 10 December 1842': Arthur Hedley, London.

    (3) Fair copy, undated: Arthur Hedley, London.

(4) Undated, but with the title-page inscribed 'à Mlle. Elise Gavard' (see **154**): Conservatoire, Paris.

(5) Fair copy: Delphine Potocka's Album, 1844: see **35**.

(6) Fair copy, undated, but signed by Chopin: Bibliothèque de l'Opéra, Paris.

(7) Fair copy (possibly one made by Fontana, and in all probability the source of Op. 70: no. 2): Conservatoire, Paris.

139

TARANTELLA in A flat major, Op. 43. Summer 1841

Publication:

Schuberth, Hamburg (449). December 1841.
Troupenas, Paris (1073). October 1841.
Wessel, London (5295). October 1841.

There is no dedication of Op. 43.

Since this work was paid for by Schuberth (500 fr.) on 1 July 1841, it is strange to read in a letter to Breitkopf & Haertel, of 29 July 1841, that the composer was still, apparently, negotiating with this firm for the publication of the Tarantella.

Wessel's publication was advertised in the *Musical World*, 28 October 1841. As an instance of the spurious dedications found in English editions of Chopin's works may be quoted that of a republication of Op. 43 by Augener: 'à mon [*sic*] ami Auguste Gathy'.

In a letter to Fontana, undated, but almost certainly of July 1841, Chopin wrote of the notation of the work and expressed the wish that it should be the same as Rossini's, in A major [*La Danza*].

MSS. (1) Fair copy: unknown. The MS. has a note in Chopin's hand with directions to Fontana to make 3 copies, writing out the repeats. None of the repeats in Chopin's MS. is fully written out. The opus number on the title-page of the autograph was left blank.

   (2) Fair copy: Conservatoire, Paris. This MS. is almost certainly one of Fontana's, and is inscribed by a former owner: 'Ex Libris August Vinens, Parisis.'

140

MAZURKA in A minor (Emil Gaillard). 1841

Publication:

   Jean Louis Chabal, Paris (erroneously as 'Op. 43'). Autumn 1841.
   Republished by:
   Bote & Bock, Berlin (3359). July 1855.

Dedicated to Emil Gaillard, a banker and a pupil of Chopin's. The composer mentions him in a letter to Mlle. Rozières, written on 3 September 1844.

The actual Op. 43 is the Tarantella in A flat (see previous item). On later issues, Chabal, a small music publisher in the Boulevard des Italiens, omitted this wrong number; one of these later issues was inscribed by Chopin to Jane Stirling.

Since this Mazurka was published so soon after being composed for Gaillard, it is possible that Chopin knew nothing of Gaillard's transaction with Chabal; the publisher, in his turn, was evidently unaware of the imminent publication of the Tarantella, and so used the opus number '43'.

MS. Lost.

141

PRELUDE in C sharp minor, Op. 45. August to September 1841

Publication:

Pietro Mechetti, Vienna (3594): in a *Beethoven Album.* November 1841.

M. Schlesinger, Paris (3518). November 1841.

Wessel, London (5297). March 1842.

Dedicated to Mlle. la Princesse Elisabeth Czernicheff (see Chopin's letter to Fontana of October 1841 for his difficulties over the spelling of her name!).

Mechetti's *Beethoven Album* was in aid of the fund for the composer's monument at Bonn. It contained ten pieces, among them, besides Chopin's Prelude, Mendelssohn's 'Variations Serieuses', Op. 54. The C sharp minor Prelude was republished by Mechetti as a separate item in 1843. On

the title-page of this edition, the Viennese publisher gives
Ewer, London, as the English publisher; this also may be
the result of unsuccessful negotiations on Ewer's part for
the publication of works by Chopin in England.

The composer wrote to Fontana on 1 October 1841: 'I
have done the C sharp minor Prelude for Schlesinger ...
tomorrow I will send you a letter for Mechetti in which
I will explain to him that if he wants a short thing for that
"Album" I will give him today's Prelude'.

To Breitkopf & Haertel he wrote on 3 December 1841:
'Mechetti in Vienna has a Prelude for his "Beethoven"
Album and a Polonaise' (see **135**).

Liszt edited this Prelude for the *Gesamtausgabe* of Breitkopf
& Haertel, the only piece in the whole edition for which he
was *de facto* responsible. A copy with revisions in several
hands and with some remarks by Brahms, is in the possession
of Antony van Hoboken, Ascona.

Wessel's edition was first advertised as *Prelude in E major*.

MS. Lost.

142

TWO NOCTURNES, Op. 48. October 1841

    No. 1 in C minor.

    No. 2 in F sharp minor.

Publication:

Breitkopf & Haertel, Leipzig (6653). January 1842: advertised in December 1841.

M. Schlesinger, Paris (3487: 3488). November 1841.

Wessel, London (5300: 5301). March 1842.

Dedicated to Mlle. Laura Duperré, a daughter of Admiral Victor Guy Duperré (1775–1846), and a favourite pupil of Chopin's.

Chopin wrote to Fontana on 10 October 1841: 'Mme. Sand's son will be in Paris about the 16th; I will send you by him the MSS. of the Concerto [Op. 46] and the Nocturnes [Op. 48].' To Breitkopf & Haertel (who paid for these nocturnes by 13 December 1841) he wrote: 'I beg you to place on the title-page of my nocturnes, instead of Mlle. Emilie, Mlle. Laura Duperré.'

Wessel's edition called the first Nocturne 'Op. 48', the second 'Op. 48: *bis*'.

MSS. Deutsche Staatsbibliothek, Berlin (now with the State Collection, Warsaw). These manuscripts contain an autograph title-page for each nocturne separately; there is a further title-page for the complete opus, headed '13me et 14me Nocturnes pour piano forte dediés à Mlle. Laure Duperré.' The first one, in C minor, is in Fontana's hand.

143

SONG for voice and PF., Op. 74: no. 8. 1841

'Śliczny chłopiec' ('Wzniosły, smukły i młody')
'Handsome Lad' ('Strong, tall and young').

(D major)

German title: 'Mein Geliebter'.
Text: Bohdan Zaleski.

No. 8

For details of the publication of Op. 74, see **32**.

MS. Lost.

144

FUGUE in A minor. 1841–1842

Publication:

> Breitkopf & Haertel, Leipzig (Klavierbibliothek: 22,707). 1898.
> (?) Metzler, Brussels and (?) G. Schirmer, New York & London. 1898.[1]

The work was announced by Breitkopf & Haertel as 'Fugue in A minor, for PF., by Fr. Chopin, revised and published according to the original manuscript in the possession of Nathalie Janotha'. She introduced, in fact, certain unjustifiable changes in the text of the fugue. Chopin has made occasional alterations and revisions in the music itself. This seems to establish it as an original composition, and not as the copy of another's work.

There is a facsimile reproduction in *Chybiński: Księga Pamiątkowa* ('Memorial Volume'), Cracow, 1950.

This A minor Fugue is not to be confused with the 'Cherubini' fugue mentioned by Niecks in his biography (English edition, Vol. I, p. 231). The 4-page MS. of a 'neat copy of one of Cherubini's fugues', said by Niecks to be in

---

[1] This fugue is said to have been published in 1877, but I have been unable to ascertain any particulars of this publication.

the possession of the descendants of Franchomme, was offered for sale by Nicolas Rauch, Geneva, in November 1958. (A facsimile reproduction of one page is given in the sale catalogue, Plate V.) It appears to consist of exercises based on subjects by Cherubini; the first page is headed by Chopin: '2 Cherubini subjects' and the fourth page '3 countersubjects'.

MS. Arthur Hedley, London.

145

THREE MAZURKAS, Op. 50. Autumn 1841 to summer 1842

> No. 1 in G major.
> No. 2 in A flat major.
> No. 3 in C sharp minor.

Publication:

> Pietro Mechetti, Vienna (3682). (June) September 1842.
> M. Schlesinger, Paris (3692). (November 1842). Spring 1843.
> Wessel, London (5303). (August 1842) October 1842.

Dedicated to Leon Szmitowski, a Polish compatriot in Paris of Chopin (who had referred to him in a letter of

September 1833, as the 'slender Szmitowski'). The English edition was dedicated by Wessel, without authorisation, to a 'Mr. Field of Bath'.

There is a possibility that the G major Mazurka was composed in 1841; Chopin wrote to Fontana on 1 October 1841 about a mazurka in Mechetti's possession 'already old'.

The dates in brackets above are of preliminary announcements. In the case of Mechetti's date there is confirmation in the Poznań journal *Literary Weekly*, but the actual publication date was probably September. Later advertisements of Schlesinger (*Gazette Musicale*) and Wessel (*Musical World*) withdrew the announcement. The final publication date in Paris is not known, but it was certainly early in 1843. Meanwhile the G major Mazurka was published alone by Schlesinger in the *Deuxième Keepsake des Pianistes*, November 1842. The *Keepsake* was an album of new pieces by Chopin, Mendelssohn, Thalberg, etc., and was issued as a supplement for subscribers to the *Gazette Musicale*.

These facts suggest that Chopin failed to compose the second and third Mazurkas in time for the publishers, for Schlesinger had prematurely announced the publication of Op. 50 as early as November 1841. They were not finished until the early summer of 1842 and are probably referred to in the composer's letter to Grzymala, undated, but of that period: 'Forgive me for asking you once more to send a letter to the Viennese publisher [Mechetti] . . . I ask the favour of you because it contains manuscripts of mine laboriously written out.'

MS. No. 3, in C sharp minor: Jagielloński Library, Cracow. Presented by Dioniz Zaleski, from the collection of the poet, Bohdan Zaleski, and a first, slightly shorter, version of the third Mazurka.

146

BALLADE no. 4, in F minor, Op. 52. 1842

Publication:

Breitkopf & Haertel, Leipzig (7001). November 1843.
M. Schlesinger, Paris (3957). December 1843.
Wessel, London (5305). (?) First advertised in April
1845.

Dedicated to Mme. la Baronne Charlotte de Rothschild,
wife of Nathaniel de Rothschild. Chopin had been introduced to the family in 1832 by Prince Valentine Radziwill.

MSS. (1) Sketch consisting of the first 79 bars, differing
from the printed version, and inscribed 'pour
Dessauer': Dr. R. F. Kallir, New York (for
Dessauer, see 90).
(2) Final version: unknown.

147

POLONAISE in A flat major, Op. 53. 1842

Publication:

Breitkopf & Haertel, Leipzig (7002). November 1843.
M. Schlesinger, Paris (3958). December 1843.
Wessel, London (5306). First advertised in April 1845.

Dedicated to Auguste Léo, Paris banker, patron of the arts, a relative of Moscheles.

For the supposed dedication to Clara Wieck: see 104.

MSS. (1) Fragment, one page consisting of bars 134–153: Alfred Cortot, Lausanne.

   (2) Complete MS: Heinemann Foundation, New York (the copy originally owned by Clara Wieck).

148

SCHERZO no. 4, in E major, Op. 54. 1842

Publication:

Breitkopf & Haertel, Leipzig (7003). November 1843.
M. Schlesinger, Paris (3959). December 1843.
Wessel, London (5307). First advertised in April 1845.

The German edition was dedicated to Mlle. Jeanne de Caraman. The composer's decision to dedicate the French edition to Mlle. Clothilde, sister of Jeanne, was made too late to prevent the first printings of the title page. This was then altered so clumsily that it had to be scrapped and the altered dedication required a new printing of the title-page.

Copies of the original page, clumsily altered, are in the possession of Arthur Hedley, London, and Antony van Hoboken, Ascona. The final title-page is reproduced in Bory's *Chopin: Vie par l'image*.

Jeanne and Clothilde de Caraman were both pupils of Chopin.

MS. Jagielloński Library, Cracow University. This MS. was originally used by Breitkopf & Haertel and contains Chopin's dedication to Jeanne de Caraman. It passed to its present owners from Edouard Ganche.

149

IMPROMPTU no. 3, in G flat major, Op. 51. ('Allegro Vivace'). Autumn 1842

Publication:

F. Hofmeister, Leipzig (2900). April 1843 (announced in February).

M. Schlesinger, Paris (3847). July 1843.

Wessel, London (5304). June 1843.

Dedicated to Mme. la Comtesse Esterházy, *née* Joanne Batthyany, born 1797, wife of Comte Alois Esterházy.

Chopin wrote to Breitkopf & Haertel on 15 December 1842: 'Besides these [Opp. 52, 53 and 54] I have written an Impromptu, of several pages, which I do not even offer to you, as I wish to oblige one of my old acquaintances, who for the last two years has been constantly asking me for something for Herr Hofmeister.' His letter assigning the Impromptu to Hofmeister and giving details of the dedication is dated 3 February 1843. He acknowledges the sum of 600 fr. from the publisher.

The work was called simply 'Allegro Vivace' in the German edition.

The Impromptu appeared in Schlesinger's *La Revue et Gazette musicale*, 9 July 1843, and was wrongly paginated. Chopin protested about this in a letter to the publisher of 22 July 1843. He asked for this correction to be published in the next issue:

Page 3 : *read* Page 5.
Page 5 : *read* Page 3.

MSS. (1) There is a first version of this Impromptu in the possession of the descendants of Chopin's young and gifted pupil, Charles Filtsch. It may possibly be the version in F♯ major, referred to by the critic Maurice Bourges, who, on 27 February 1842, wrote of a recital in Paris given by Chopin and mentioned an 'Impromptu in F♯ major'.

(2) Fair copy: unknown, formerly in the Wilhelm Heyer Collection, Cologne. The autograph is headed simply '*Tempo giusto*'.

150

WALTZ in A minor. (?) 1843

Publication:

La Revue Musicale (Éditions Richard-Masse), Paris. Facsimile reproductions of the two MSS. are included, and there is a foreword by Suzanne and Denise Chainaye. May 1955.

The Waltz was probably composed for Mme. Charlotte de Rothschild, or her daughter. The MSS. (see below) were given to the Paris Conservatoire by a member of the Rothschild family in 1901.

J. G. Prod'homme, in the *Musical Quarterly*, New York, January 1939, referred to the Waltz as 'a youthful work'. It was first described by the present writer in the *Monthly Musical Record*, March 1955, where the *incipit* was quoted to preclude any possible confusion with the A minor Waltz, Op. 34: no. 2.

MSS. (1) Rough draft.
   (2) Fair copy, entitled 'Walc'.
      Both manuscripts: Conservatoire, Paris.

151

MODERATO in E major ('Albumblatt'). 1843

Publication:

The periodical *Świat*, Warsaw, 4 June 1910, no. 23, page 8, edited by Henryk Pachulski.
Republished by:
Gebethner & Wolff, Warsaw, 1927, for the Warsaw Committee collecting funds for the Chopin Monument. (P. N. 5203.)

Written in the Album of Countess Anna Szeremetieff. The piece is known as 'Albumblatt'. It has been called a Prelude by Ferdinand Hoesick, and a Nocturne by Zdisłav Jachimecki.

MS. Anna Szeremetieff's Album, inscribed 'F. F. Chopin, Paris, 1843': unknown.

152

TWO NOCTURNES, Op. 55. 1843
   No. 1 in F minor.
   No. 2 in E flat major.

Publication:

    Breitkopf & Haertel, Leipzig (7142). August 1844.
    M. Schlesinger, Paris (4084). August 1844.
    Wessel, London (5308). First advertised in April 1845.

Dedicated to Jane Wilhelmina Stirling (1804–1859), younger daughter of John Stirling of Kippendavie and a pupil of Chopin. A copy of the French edition with the dedication to Jane Stirling in the composer's hand is in the Paris Conservatoire.

The contemporary handwritten copy of these Nocturnes in the Jagielloński Library, Cracow University, may be in the hand of Franchomme.

MSS. (1) No. 1, in F minor: Conservatoire, Paris.
      (2) Nos. 1 and 2: Chopin Institute, Warsaw, with the dedication in the composer's hand.

153

THREE MAZURKAS, Op. 56. 1843

    No. 1 in B major.
    No. 2 in C major.
    No. 3 in C minor.

Publication:

   Breitkopf & Haertel, Leipzig (7143). August 1844.
   M. Schlesinger, Paris (4085). August 1844.
   Wessel, London (5309). First advertised in April 1845.

Dedicated to Catherine Maberly, a friend of Jane Stirling and a pupil of Chopin.

MSS. (1) No. 2, in C major, first sketch on one page: British Museum (originally with Marcelline Czartoryska, then with E. H. W. Meyerstein).

    (2) A second sketch for No. 2, in C major: unknown. This was reproduced in Kleczyński's *Chopin's Greater Works*, 1883, and shows Chopin's original penultimate bars to have consisted of a three-bar trill on a bass octave on the dominant. The MS. was again reproduced by Leichentritt in 1905.

    (3) The complete opus: Chopin Institute, Warsaw.

154

B ERCEUSE in D flat major, Op. 57. 1843, revised in 1844

Publication:

>Breitkopf & Haertel, Leipzig (7259). (May) July 1845.
>
>J. Meissonnier, Paris (2186). July 1845.
>
>Wessel, London (6313). June 1845.

Dedicated to Mlle. Elise Gavard, a pupil of Chopin's. Her brother, Charles Gavard, was an acquaintance of the composer in his last years and wrote reminiscences of him after his death. The dedication in Chopin's hand 'à Mlle. Elise Gavard, son vieux professeur et ami, F. F. Chopin', on a separate page, is in the Paris Conservatoire.

The Berceuse was played by the composer on 2 February 1844, and revised at Nohant, the country residence of George Sand, later in the year. The journal *Gazette Musicale*, 5 January 1845, no. 1, page 6, referred to the Sonata in B minor (see next) and the Berceuse when it reported Chopin's arrival in Paris from Nohant:

>'Chopin est de retour à Paris; il rapporta une nouvelle grande sonate et des variantes. Bientôt ces deux importants ouvrages seront publiés.'

The term 'variantes' must have originated from the composer himself, and is justified by the MS. sketch in the possession of M. Alfred Cortot (MS. (1) below).

The Berceuse and the Sonata in B minor were published in Paris by Meissonnier, and not Schlesinger, apparently because the latter wished to postpone publication against the composer's wishes (see his letters of 1 and 2 August 1844 to Franchomme.)

Wessel's edition of the Berceuse is the only one in his complete series on which he printed the names of both continental publishers.

MSS. (1) First sketch, showing an embryonic 'variation' form: Alfred Cortot, Lausanne.

>(2) Chopin Institute, Warsaw.
>
>(3) Conservatoire, Paris. This 'definitive' text, as it has been called, still lacks the two introductory bars.

SONATA no. 2, in B minor, Op. 58. Summer 1844

Publication:

Breitkopf & Haertel, Leipzig (7260). (May) July 1845.
J. Meissonnier, Paris (2187). July 1845.
Wessel, London (6314). June 1845.

Dedicated to Mme. la Comtesse E. de Perthuis (see **89**); she is referred to as 'Perthuis' amiable wife'.

Brahms edited the Sonata for Breitkopf's 'Gesamtausgabe' (Vol. VIII).

There is an autograph copy of this Sonata made by Liszt, with his variant for the finale, in the Rocheblave Collection, Paris.

MSS. (1) Sketches: with the descendants of Franchomme.
     (2) Chopin Institute, Warsaw.

156

Two Songs for voice and PF., Op. 74: nos. 11 and 13. 1845

> No. 11 'Dwojaki koniec' ('Rok się kochali . . .')
>   'The Double End' ('They loved for a year . . .').
>
> (D minor)

German title: 'Zwei Leichen'.

> No. 13 'Nie ma czego trzeba' ('Mgła mi do oczu')
>   'I want what I have not' ('Mist before my eyes').
>
> (A minor)

German title: 'Melancholie'.

The texts of both songs are by Bohdan Zaleski.

For details of the publication of Op. 74, see **32**.

No. 13 is sometimes called 'Dumka' (see **132**).

MSS. Lost.

157

THREE MAZURKAS, Op. 59. June to July 1845

    No. 1 in A minor.
    No. 2 in A flat major.
    No. 3 in F sharp minor.

Publication:

    Stern, Berlin (71). November 1845.
    Brandus (successor to M. Schlesinger), Paris (4292).
    March 1846.
    Wessel, London (6315). December 1845.

There is no dedication of Op. 59.

Chopin wrote to his family on 20 July 1845 '. . . I have written three new mazurkas which will probably come out in Berlin, because a man I know has begged me for them: Stern, a good fellow and a learned musician, whose father is starting a music shop there.' Stern's business was purchased by Friedländer, Berlin, in 1852.

Schlesinger's business was acquired by Brandus early in

1846. One of these Mazurkas was given as a supplement to Schlesinger's *Revue et Gazette Musicale* on 24 May 1846, entitled '*Mazurka Nouvelle* de Chopin'.

For Wessel's so-called 'Op. 59: *bis*', see 134.

MSS. (1) No. 2, in A flat major: Bibliothèque de l'Opéra, Paris.

     (2) No. 3, in F sharp minor: there is a first sketch for this Mazurka in G minor. The manuscript was formerly in the Peters' Music Library. See *Jahrbuch der Musikbibliothek*, 1934.

     (3) No. 3, in F sharp minor: Mrs. Eva Alberman, London. This copy, headed simply 'No. 3', was once owned by Hans von Bülow together with the other two mazurkas of this opus. He gave No. 3 on 2 November 1864 to C. Kerfack from whom it passed first to the Wilhelm Heyer Collection, Cologne, and thence to its present owner.

158

BARCAROLLE in F sharp major, Op. 60. Autumn 1845 to summer 1846

Publication:

    Breitkopf & Haertel, Leipzig (7545). November 1846.
    Brandus, Paris (4609). November 1846.
    Wessel, London (6317). September 1846.

Dedicated to Mme. la Baronne de Stockhausen (see **66**).

MSS. (1) Cracow University (former owner, Baron de Stockhausen 1877; it passed to its present owners from Edouard Ganche.)

(2) Mrs. Eva Alberman, London.

159

POLONAISE-FANTASIE in A flat major, Op. 61. Autumn 1845 to summer 1846

Publication:

Breitkopf & Haertel, Leipzig (7546). November 1846.
Brandus, Paris (4610). November 1846.
Wessel, London (6318). October 1846.

Dedicated to Mme. A. Veyret, a mutual acquaintance of Chopin and George Sand (see the composer's letter to George Sand of 12 December 1847).

Chopin wrote to his family on 12 December 1845: '. . . I should like now to finish my violoncello sonata, barcarole and something else I don't know how to name . . .'—a reference to the Polonaise-Fantasie.

Wessel's edition was on sale in London in October 1846.

MSS. (1) Chopin Institute, Warsaw: originally with Breitkopf.

(2) State Collection, Warsaw.

SONATA in G minor, for PF. and cello, Op. 65. Autumn 1845–1846

Publication:

> Breitkopf & Haertel, Leipzig (7718). January 1848.
> Brandus, Paris (4744). October 1847.

Dedicated to Auguste Franchomme (1808–1884), eminent French cellist and close friend of Chopin in the latter years of the composer's life.

Chopin wrote to his family on 11 October 1846: '. . . with

my Sonata for cello I am now contented, now discontented.'
He wrote again in April 1847: '. . . I played her [Delphine
Potocka] my violoncello sonata with Franchomme, in my
lodging.' (See also note to previous item.)

The Sonata was not published in England until the Paris
Edition of Richault in 1860 (see Appendix III).

Breitkopf & Haertel announced the publication of the
work in September 1847. Shortly after its actual publication,
they published an arrangement for PF. and Violin, by
Ferdinand David.

Brandus, in the *Revue et Gazette Musicale*, 17 October 1847,
advertised this work, together with Opp. 63 and 64, as 'to
appear immediately'. The PF. solo arrangement, published
by Brandus, is by Moscheles.

MSS. (1) Sketch of the first movement: Conservatoire,
        Paris.
     (2) One leaf of the first movement, and the Finale,
        headed 'Nohant, 1846': Mme. Edouard André (a
        descendant of Franchomme).
     (3) Fragmentary sketches for a (? different) Scherzo,
        seventeen bars: J. A. Stargardt, Marburg, 13 May
        1958.

160 (B)

Two Bourrées, written down by Chopin. (?) 1846

    No. 1 in G major.
    No. 2 in A major.

Unpublished. A facsimile reproduction was given in the
catalogue of sale (see MS. below).

These airs were notated for the pianoforte and given a simple harmonisation by Chopin while he was at Nohant. They are supposed to be dance tunes native to Berry and were used by George Sand for the music in her play *François le Champi*.

MS. A music Album of George Sand: Maurice Rheim, Paris, June 1957.

161

Two Nocturnes, Op. 62. 1846

No. 1 in B major.
No. 2 in E major.

Publication:

Breitkopf & Haertel, Leipzig (7547). November 1846.
Brandus, Paris (4611). November 1846.
Wessel, London (6319). October 1846.

Dedicated to Mlle. R. de Könneritz, a pupil of Chopin who later married Herr von Heygendorf. Copies of the pieces she studied with Chopin, corrected in his hand, were used as the basis of Peters's *Complete Edition* (1879). The dedication represents the composer's second thoughts: his first choice is vigorously scratched out from the MS. ((3) below).

The second of these nocturnes was republished in 1847 by the *La Revue Musicale* in their 'Album des Pianistes'.

MSS. (1) No. 2, in E major, Arthur Hedley, London.

    (2) Both nocturnes: Chopin Institute, Warsaw. This MS. was originally with Brandus and contains the 'clean' dedication. It is reproduced in facsimile in the 'Nocturnes' volume (VII) of the Polish 'Complete Edition'.

    (3) Both nocturnes: Newberry Library, Chicago (from the descendants of W. Grzymala). This MS. contains the cancelled first dedication; it is reproduced in facsimile in Bory's *Chopin: Vie par l'image*.

162

THREE MAZURKAS, Op. 63. Early autumn 1846

    No. 1 in B major.
    No. 2 in F minor.
    No. 3 in C sharp minor.

Publication:

    Breitkopf & Haertel, Leipzig (7714). November 1847.
    Brandus, Paris (4742). October 1847.
    Wessel, London (No 'Publisher's Number' printed). December 1847.

Dedicated to Mme. la Comtesse Laura de Czosnowska.

Chopin referred to the composition of these three mazurkas in his letter to his family of 11 October 1846.

Breitkopf & Haertel announced publication on 8 September 1847.

Wessel's edition contained no Publisher's Number, but from the ones allotted to neighbouring opus numbers it should have been '6320'. The three mazurkas were pirated by Cramer & Beale, London, who published them in June 1848.

On the French edition Jullien, London, is given as the English publisher [Louis Antoine Jullien]: this reveals further unsuccessful negotiations for the copyright of Chopin's works in England, and shows what difficulties Wessel was up against in his efforts to retain the right of being Chopin's sole publisher in England.

MSS. (1) Sketch of No. 1, in B major, headed 'Nohant, 1846': Conservatoire, Paris.

      A facsimile reproduction of this MS. was given in the *Catalogue for the Chopin Centenary Exhibition* (1949) of the Bibliothèque Nationale, Paris.

  (2) No. 2, in F minor, written in the album of René, Franchomme's little son: unknown.

163

MAZURKA in A minor, Op. 67: no. 4 (Posth.). 1846

The mazurka exists in three versions.

Publication:

Version (*a*): For details of the publication of Op. 67, see **93**.

(*b*): *Dans le Souvenir de Frédéric Chopin*, Edouard Ganche, Paris, 1925, page 236. This was the basis of the version in the *Oxford Edition of Chopin's Works*, London, 1932, vol. III.

(*c*): Polish 'Complete Edition', 1956, vol. X, no. 47, *bis*: from MS. (3) below.

This is possibly a mazurka rejected from the collection for Op. 63 (previous item). The date is according to Fontana.

A copy of the Mazurka, made by Thomas Tellefsen in May 1850, for Marcelline Czartoryska: unknown.

MSS. (1) Version (*a*): Lost.

(2) Version (*b*): unknown, formerly with Edouard Ganche.

(3) Version (*c*): 'Gesellschaft der Musikfreunde', Vienna (originally in the possession of Brahms. It is dated 'Paris, 1848'.)

164

THREE WALTZES, Op. 64. 1846–1847

No. 1 in D flat major.
No. 2 in C sharp minor.
No. 3 in A flat major.

Publication:

> Breitkopf & Haertel, Leipzig: the three waltzes separately (7715, 7716, 7717); the complete set (7721). November 1847.
> Brandus, Paris (4743: 1, 2 and 3). October 1847.
> Cramer & Beale, London. Op. 64: nos. 1 and 2 only (4368, 4369). April 1848.
> Wessel, London (6321, 6322, 6323). September 1848.

Dedications in the French edition only:

> No. 1, in D flat major: Countess Delphine Potocka (see 44).
> No. 2, in C sharp minor: Baroness de Rothschild (see 146).
> No. 3, in A flat major: Countess Catherine de Branicka, of the exiled Polish aristocracy in Paris, a pupil of Chopin's. Early editions wrongly gave this dedication to Baroness Bronicka.

Cramer & Beale's edition was pirated. They published the third waltz later as 'Op. 64: 3'. The French edition again gives the name of Jullien, London, as the English publisher (see 162).

Wessel may have published the complete opus after he found that Cramer & Beale had published part of it; his publication of Op. 64 undoubtedly took place in September 1848: the acquisition date on the copy in the British Museum is 20 September 1848. It is clear from his publisher's number that the work was put into preparation at the same time as Op. 63.

The Waltz in D flat major is the so-called 'Minute' Waltz.

MSS. (1) No. 1, in D flat major, first version: Conservatoire, Paris.
　　　(2) No. 1, second version: Conservatoire, Paris.

(3) No. 2, in C sharp minor, first version: Conservatoire, Paris. This MS. was bequeathed to the
Conservatoire library by Baroness Charlotte de
Rothschild. It was first published in the *Oxford
Edition of Chopin's Works*, vol. I, 1932. In this
version the anacrusis (crotchet on the third beat
of the first bar) is omitted by Chopin.

(4) No. 2 and no. 3, in A flat major, first sketches (the
second originally with Marcelline Czartoryska):
Bibliothèque de l'Opéra, Paris.

165

SONG for voice and PF., Op. 74: no. 9. 1847

'Melodya' ('Z gór gdzie dźwigali strasznych krzyżów')
'Melody' ('From the mountains they bore the terrible
crosses').

(G major/E minor)

German title: 'Eine Melodie'.

Text: Zygmunt Krasiński. Early editions of the song give
'Author unknown'.

For details of the publication of Op. 74, see **32**.

MS. Delphine Potocka's Album: below his signature
Chopin is said to have written 'Nella miseria', from
Dante's celebrated lines in Canto V, 121 of the *Inferno*:

> Nessun maggior dolore
> Che ricordarsi del tempo felice
> Nella miseria.

166

WALTZ in B major. 12 October 1848

Unpublished

The Waltz was written for Mrs. Erskine, Jane Stirling's elder sister. It was discovered in 1952 by Mr. Arthur Hedley. MS. Arthur Hedley, London.

167

MAZURKA in G minor, Op. 67: no. 2 (Posth.). Summer 1849

For details of the publication of Op. 67, see **93**.

In Louise's list this Mazurka is dated '1848'.

MS. Lost.

168

MAZURKA in F minor, Op. 68: no. 4 (Posth.). Summer 1849

For details of the publication of Op. 68, see **18**, and also note below.

In Louise's list this Mazurka is dated '1848'. According to Fontana this is Chopin's last composition. But it is not the final version from Chopin's pen, being, in fact, a mazurka 'realised' by August Franchomme from Chopin's sketches, in June 1852 (see *Souvenirs inédits de Chopin*, page 196). Arthur Hedley discovered the original MS. version in the papers of the Lemire-André family, descendants of Franchomme. It contains an episode in F major, omitted by Franchomme in his 'realisation'.

A. M. Schlesinger, Berlin, published the piece separately in 1852, as the *Dernière Pensée Musicale Mazurka*, that is, three years before Fontana's posthumous publication of Op. 68.

MS. Sketches: Lemire-André family, Paris.

Appendix I

CHRONOLOGICAL SEQUENCE OF PUBLICATION

1817
....   Military March (lost).
November   Polonaise in G minor (republ. 1927).

1825
June   Rondo, Op. 1.

1826
....   Mazurkas in B flat and G (2nd versions: republ. 1851).
          Polonaise in B flat minor (republ. 1879).

1828
February   Rondo à la Mazur, Op. 5.

1830
January   Variations for PF. and Orch., Op. 2.

1831
Autumn   Introduction and Polonaise, Op. 3.

1832
December   PF. Trio in G minor, Op. 8.
          3 Nocturnes, Op. 9.
          4 Mazurkas, Op. 6.
          5 Mazurkas, Op. 7.

1833
July   Études, Op. 10.
          PF. Concerto, Op. 11.
          Grand Duo (*Robert le Diable*).
November   Variations (*Ludovic*), Op. 12.
December   3 Nocturnes, Op. 15.

1834

March	Introduction and Rondo, Op. 16.
	4 Mazurkas, Op. 17.
April	Fantasia on Polish Airs, Op. 13.
June	Waltz, Op. 18.
July	Rondo, 'Krakowiak', Op. 14.
October	Bolero, Op. 19.

1835

February	Scherzo, Op. 20.

1836

January	4 Mazurkas, Op. 24.
April	PF. Concerto, Op. 21.
May	2 Nocturnes, Op. 27.
June	Ballade, Op. 23.
July	2 Polonaises, Op. 26.
August	*Andante spianato* and Polonaise, Op. 22.
....	2 Songs ('Życzenie' and 'Wojak'), publ. anonymously.

1837

October	Études, Op. 25.
December	4 Mazurkas, Op. 30.
	Scherzo, Op. 31.
	2 Nocturnes, Op. 32.

1838

October	4 Mazurkas, Op. 33.
December	3 Waltzes, Op. 34.

1839

June	*Hexameron*, Variation in E major.
	Preludes, Op. 28.

1840

May	Sonata, Op. 35.
	Impromptu, Op. 36.
June	2 Nocturnes, Op. 37.
	Waltz in A flat, Op. 42.
September	Ballade, Op. 38.
October	Scherzo, Op. 39.
November	Trois Nouvelles Études.

December   2 Polonaises, Op. 40.
                4 Mazurkas, Op. 41.

1841

October   Mazurka in A minor (Emil Gaillard).
                Tarantella, Op. 43.
November Polonaise, Op. 44.
                Prelude, Op. 45.
                Allegro de Concert, Op. 46.
                Ballade, Op. 47.
                2 Nocturnes, Op. 48.
                Fantasia in F minor, Op. 49.

1842

February   Mazurka in A minor (*Notre Temps*).
September 3 Mazurkas, Op. 50.

1843

April   Impromptu, Op. 51.
November Ballade, Op. 52.
                Polonaise, Op. 53.
                Scherzo, Op. 54.

1844

August   2 Nocturnes, Op. 55.
                3 Mazurkas, Op. 56.

1845

June   Berceuse, Op. 57.
                Sonata, Op. 58.
November 3 Mazurkas, Op. 59.

1846

October   Barcarolle, Op. 60.
                Polonaise-Fantasia, Op. 61.
                2 Nocturnes, Op. 62.

1847

October   3 Mazurkas, Op. 63.
                3 Waltzes, Op. 64.
                Sonata for PF. and cello, Op. 65.

Posthumous publication:

1851

May   'Schweizerbub' Variations.
Sonata, Op. 4.

1852

....   'Deux Valses Mélancholiques' (Op. 70: no. 2; Op. 69: no. 2).

1855

May   Fantasie-Impromptu, Op. 66.
4 Mazurkas, Op. 67.
4 Mazurkas, Op. 68.
2 Waltzes, Op. 69.
3 Waltzes, Op. 70.
3 Polonaises, Op. 71.
Nocturne, Funeral March, 3 Écossaises, Op. 72.
Rondo for 2 pianofortes, Op. 73.

1856

....   2 songs republ. with Chopin's name, from 1836.

1857

....   16 Polish songs, Op. 74.

1859–1860

....   16 Songs, with German translations, Op. 74.

1864

....   Polonaise in G sharp minor.

1868

....   Waltz in E minor.

1870

....   Polonaise in G flat major.
Mazurka in C major.
Song ('Polens Grabgesang'), Op. 74: no. 17.

1871

....   Waltz in E major.

1875

January	Nocturne (*Lento con gran espressione*).
	Mazurka in D major (1st version).
	Mazurkas in B flat and G (1st versions).

1879

....	Mazurka in G ('Prague').

1880

January	Mazurka in D major (2nd version).

1881

....	Variations in A major (on a theme by Paganini).

1898

....	Fugue in A minor.

1902

....	Polonaise in A flat (corrupt: republ. 'clean' in 1908).
	Waltz in A flat.
	Waltz in E flat.
	Mazurka in A minor (1st version), Op. 7: no. 2.

1909

....	Mazurka in B flat (Alexandra Wolowska).

1910

February	Mazurka ('Mazurek') in D major.
	Song: 'Czary'.
June	Moderato in E major (republ. 1927).
October	Song: 'Dumka'.

1918

August	Prelude in A flat (Pierre Wolff).

1930

....	Mazurka in A flat (Celina Szymanowska).

1931

....	Cantabile in B flat major.

1934

.... Contredanse in G flat major.
Polonaise in B flat major (republ. in 1937).

1938

.... Nocturne in C minor.
Largo in E flat.

1954

.... Rondo (1st version of Op. 73).

1955

May Waltz in A minor.
Waltz in E flat.

Appendix II

PUBLISHERS OF THE FIRST EDITIONS

A. ENGLAND

London Wessel & Co.

Opp. 1–3, 5–11, 13–64; *Notre Temps* Mazurka; 'Deux Valses Mélancholiques' (Op. 70: no. 2, Op. 69: no. 2); 'Emil Gaillard' Mazurka.

Cocks.

Op. 4, 'Schweizerbub' Variations.

Cramer, Addison & Beale.

Op. 12, *Hexameron* Variation, in E.

Francis, Day & Hunter.

Waltz in E flat.

Stanley Lucas, Weber.

Op. 74.

B. FRANCE

Paris Maurice Schlesinger.

Opp. 1, 2, 6–18, 20–27, 29–34, 44–56; 'Grand Duo'; Trois Nouvelles Études.

Brandus (successor to Schlesinger).

Opp. 59–65.

Eugene Troupenas.

Opp. 35–41, 43; *Notre Temps* Mazurka.

Joseph Meissonnier.

Opp. 57, 58.

Joseph Meissonnier fils.

Opp. 66–73.

Adolph Catelin et Cie.

Op. 28.

Antonio F. G. Pacini.

Op. 42.

Prillip et Cie.

Op. 19.

Simon Richault.
Opp. 3, 4; 'Schweizerbub' Variations.

Schonenberger.
Op. 5.

Chabal.
'Emil Gaillard' Mazurka.

Revue Musicale.
Waltz in A minor.

J. Hamelle.
Op. 74.

C. GERMANY AND AUSTRIA

Leipzig Breitkopf & Haertel.
Opp. 12, 15–18, 20–31, 33–42, 46–49, 52–58, 60–65;
Waltzes in A flat and E flat; Mazurka in D major (two
versions).

H. A. Probst-Kistner.
Opp. 6–11, 13 and 14.

Peters.
Op. 19.

Hofmeister.
Opp. 5 and 51.

Mainz B. Schott's Sons.
Polonaises in G sharp minor and G flat; *Notre Temps* Mazurka,
Mazurka in C, Waltz in E minor.

Berlin Adolf Martin Schlesinger (after 1844: Heinrich, son; after
1865: Robert Lienau).
Opp. 1, 32, 66–74; 'Grand Duo'; Trois Nouvelles Études.

Stern & Co.
Op. 59.

Bote & Bock.
'Emil Gaillard' Mazurka.

Hamburg Schuberth & Co.
Op. 43.

Vienna Tobias Haslinger (after 1844: his widow; after 1849: Karl,
son).
Op. 2; 'Schweizerbub' Variations.

Pietro Mechetti.
Opp. 3, 44, 45 and 50.

D. POLAND

Cracow   W. Chaberski.
Waltz in E major.
J. Wildt.
'Deux Valses Mélancholiques' (Op. 70: no. 2, Op. 69: no. 2).
S. A. Krzyańowski.
Polonaises in A flat and B flat.

Lwow   *Lamus*, 1909.
Mazurka in B flat.

Poznań   J. Leitgeber.
'Lento con gran espressione'; Mazurka in D major (1st version).

Warsaw   J. J. Cybulski.
Polonaise in G minor.
Andrea Brzezina & Co.
Opp. 1 and 5.
R. Friedlein.
Mazurkas in B flat and G major.
Gebethner & Wolff.
Mazurka in A flat; Op. 74; *Moderato* in E major.
J. Kauffmann.
Waltz in E minor; Mazurka in C major; Polonaises in G sharp minor and G flat major.
Echo Muzyczne, 1881.
Variations in A major (on a theme by Paganini).
Muzyka, 1931.
Cantabile in B flat major.

E. SWITZERLAND

Geneva   *Pages d'Art*, 1918.
Prelude in A flat major.

Appendix III

COMPLETE EDITIONS

THE following list is selective; only those complete editions with some claim to having been based on original material, have been included. The order is chronological.

1. Wessel & Co., London. *c.* 1853

'Wessel & Co. Complete Collection of the Compositions of Frederic Chopin for the Piano-Forte.' (For the 71 items in this collection, see Appendix IV).

The first and most complete of all the nineteenth century 'Complete Editions' prior to that of Breitkopf & Haertel, 1878–1880.

2. Simon Richault, Paris. 1860

'New and cheap Paris edition. The Works of Frédéric Chopin.' Edited by Thomas Tellefsen. 12 volumes, excluding the songs.

Tellefsen (1823–1874) was a pupil of Chopin's for a short time.

[Schonenberger, Paris. 1860. Vols. 21–24 of the publisher's 'Bibliothèque Classique des Pianistes' were devoted to the PF. Works of Chopin. They were called 'Oeuvres Completes' and were supplied with a biography and analyses by Fètis père, but it was not, in fact, a complete collection.]

3. Gebethner, Warsaw. 1863

'Frédéric Chopin: oeuvres pour le piano, edition originale. Varsovie, 1863.'

The edition was authorised by the composer's family. There were no songs. It was revised in 1877 and published in six volumes by the firm, now Gebethner & Wolff. It contained all the opus numbers, up to Op. 73, with the exception of Op. 65, and it was arranged numerically by opus numbers. The songs were added in 1880.

A third edition, edited by Jan Kleczyński, and containing various supplementary works, was published in 1882, in ten volumes.

4. P. Jurgenson, Moscow. 1873–1876

'Complete works of Chopin, critically revised after the original French, German and Polish editions, by Karl Klindworth.' The edition contained PF. works only, and was in six volumes.

Klindworth (1830–1916) was a pupil of Liszt.

5. Breitkopf & Haertel, Leipzig. 1878–1880

'First critically revised complete edition, edited by Woldemar Bargiel, Johannes Brahms, Auguste Franchomme, Franz Liszt, Carl Reinecke, Ernst Rudorff.'

The songs were translated by Hans Schmidt. This was the most complete edition to date, and contained 213 items in 14 volumes. It replaced a slightly earlier, but inferior 'complete edition' by this firm, edited by Carl Reinecke, and called *Neue Revidirte Ausgabe*, in ten volumes.

A supplement, containing the Waltzes in A flat and E flat, and the first version of the A minor Mazurka, Op. 7: no. 2, was added in 1902.

6. F. Kistner, Leipzig. 1879

'Fréd. Chopin's works, revised and fingered (for the most part according to the composer's notes) by Karl Mikuli.'
17 volumes.

Mikuli (1821–1888) was a pupil of Chopin's from 1844–1848; he was assisted in preparing this edition by his fellow-pupil Friedericke Streicher (*née* Müller).

7. C. F. Peters, Leipzig. 1879

'Fr. Chopin's Collected Works.' 12 volumes.

This was edited by Hermann Scholtz (d. 1918). He used the autographs of Op. 7: no. 3, Opp. 28, 48, 51 and 54, and a sketch of Op. 30: no. 4. He also used various printed editions which had been corrected by Chopin for his pupils Frau von Heygendorf (*née* Könneritz) and Georg Mathias.

8. Oxford University Press, London. 1932

The Oxford Original Edition of Fr. Chopin. Edited by Edouard Ganche, Président de la Société Fr. Chopin, à Paris. 3 volumes, PF. works only.

The edition was based on original French editions belonging to Jane Stirling, corrected in Chopin's hand. They went to Ganche from Mrs. Anne D. Houston, a great-niece of Jane Stirling's. There are prefaces in English, French and German.

9. Polish Complete Edition, Warsaw. 1937–

'Complete Works of Frederick Chopin.' ('Dzieła Wszystkie Fryderyk Chopina'), edited by Ignaz Paderewski, Ludwig Broñarski and Josef Turczyński. 26 volumes.

The edition is based on original MSS. and first editions, with a supplementary 'Editors' Report' to each volume. The project was inspired in 1937 by the Frédéric Chopin Institute of Warsaw, and the Polish Music Publishers' Association of Cracow.

The last eight volumes are to consist of full scores and parts. There are prefaces in Polish to all volumes, and English, French and Russian editions of these are gradually appearing.

Appendix IV

WESSEL'S COMPLETE EDITION

THE following list shows the numbering of each item in the English edition. The appropriate numbers were filled in by hand in the early years, later they were hand-printed.

Nº 1.	'Adieu à Varsovie' *Rondeau*	Op.	1
2.	'Hommage à Mozart' *Grandes Var. brill.* on 'LA CI DAREM' *from Don Giovanni*	Op.	2
3.	'La Gaieté' *Intr. et Polonoise brillante*	Op.	3
4.	'La Posiana' *Rondeau à la Mazur*	Op.	5
5.	'Souvenir de la Pologne' 1st set of mazurkas	Op.	6
6.	2nd set of mazurkas	Op.	7
7.	'Murmures de la Seine' 1st set of Notturnos	Op.	9
8.	2nd set of Noturnos	Op.	9
9.	'Douze grandes Études' Bk. 1	Op.	10
10.	Bk. 2	Op.	10
XI [*sic*]	'First Grand Concerto'	Op.	11
12.	'Fantasie brillante' *sur des airs nationaux polonois*	Op.	13
13.	'Krakovia' *Grand Rondeau de Concert*	Op.	14
14.	'Les Zephyrs' 3rd set of Notturnos	Op.	15
15.	'Rondo Élégant'	Op.	16
16.	'Souvenirs de la Pologne' 3rd set of mazurkas	Op.	17
17.	'Invitation pour la danse' *Grande* Valse	Op.	18
18.	'Souvenir d'Andalousie' *Bolero*	Op.	19
19.	'Le Banquet' 1st Scherzo	Op.	20
20.	'Second Grand Concerto'	Op.	21
21.	'Grand polonoise brillante' *precedée d'un Andante spianato*	Op.	22
22.	'La Favorite' *Ballade (ohne Worte)*	Op.	23
23.	'Souvenir de la Pologne' 4th set of mazurkas	Op.	24
24.	'Douze Études' 3rd set of Studies	Op.	25
25.	Idem 4th set of Studies	Op.	25
26.	'Les Favorites' *Deux Polonoises*	Op.	26
27.	'Les Plaintives' 4th set of Notturnos	Op.	27
28.	'Twenty-four grand Preludes' *through all keys* 5th set of Studies	Op.	28
29.	6th set of Studies	Op.	28

30.	'First Impromptu'		Op. 29
31.	'Souvenir de la Pologne'	5th set of mazurkas	Op. 30
32.	'Second Scherzo'		Op. 31
33.	'Il Lamento e la Consolazione'	5th set of Notturnos	Op. 32
34.	'Souvenir de la Pologne'	6th set of mazurkas	Op. 33
35.	'Trois Grandes Valses'	B^k. 1	Op. 34
36.	....	B^k. 2	Op. 34
37.	....	B^k. 3	Op. 34
38.	'Grande Sonate'		Op. 35
39.	'Second Impromptu'		Op. 36
40.	'Les Soupirs' 6th set of Notturnos		Op. 37
41.	'La Gracieuse' *2de Ballade (ohne Worte)*		Op. 38
42.	'Third Scherzo'		Op. 39
43.	'Les Favorites' *Deux Polonoises (Set 2)*		Op. 40
44.	'Souvenir de la Pologne'	7th set of mazurkas	Op. 41
45.	'Grande Valse'		Op. 42
46.	'Tarantelle'		Op. 43
47.	'Grand Polonoise'		Op. 44
48.	'Prelude' [in E [*sic*]]		Op. 45
49.	'Allegro *de* Concert'		Op. 46
50.	'Third Ballade'		Op. 47
51.	'Thirteenth Nocturne'		Op. 48
52.	'Fourteenth Nocturne'		Op. 48 *bis*
53.	'Grand Fantasia'		Op. 49
54.	'Souvenir de la Pologne'	8th set of mazurkas	Op. 50
55.	'Third Impromptu'		Op. 51
56.	'Fourth Ballade'		Op. 52
57.	'Eighth Polonaise'		Op. 53
58.	'Fourth Scherzo'		Op. 54
59.	'15me & 16me Nocturno'		Op. 55
60.	'Souvenirs de la Pologne'	9th set of mazurkas	Op. 56
61.	'La Berceuse' *Andante*		Op. 57
62.	'Second Grand Sonata'		Op. 58
63.	'Souvenirs de la Pologne'	10th set of mazurkas	Op. 59
64.	'Cracow' *Mazurka*		Op. 59 *bis*
65.	'Barcarolle'		Op. 60
66.	'Polonaise Fantaisie'		Op. 61
67.	'17me & 18me Nocturno'		Op. 62
68.	'Souvenirs de la Pologne'	11th set of mazurkas	Op. 63
69.	'Deux Valses'	N° 1	
70.	D^o	N° 2	Op. 64
71.	'Valse'	N° 3	

Appendix V

DEDICATIONS

Agoult, Marie, Comtesse d'	- 12 Studies, Op. 25.
Albrecht, Thomas - -	- Scherzo, Op. 20.
Apponyi, Comtesse d' -	- 2 Nocturnes, Op. 27.
Beauvais, Princesse Ludmilla de	- Polonaise, Op. 44.
Belgiojoso, Princesse Christine de	*Hexameron* Variation in E major.
Billing, Baronne de - -	- 2 Nocturnes, Op. 32.
Branicka, Comtesse Catherine de	- Waltz, Op. 64: no. 3.
Caraman, Clothilde de -	- Scherzo, Op. 54 (French Edition).
Caraman, Jeanne de - -	- Scherzo, Op. 54 (German Edition).
Czartoryska, Princess Adam	- 'Krakowiak' Rondo, Op. 14.
Czernicheff, Princess Elisabeth	- Prelude, Op. 45.
Czosnowska, Countess Laura de	- 3 Mazurkas, Op. 63.
Dessauer, Josef - - -	- 2 Polonaises, Op. 26.
Duperré, Mlle. Laura -	- 2 Nocturnes, Op. 48.
Dupont, Mme. (?) Sofie -	- Polonaise in G sharp minor.
Eichtal, Mlle. A. d' - -	- Waltz, Op. 34: no. 3.
Elsner, Josef - - -	- Sonata, Op. 4 (Posth.).
Elsner, Emily - - -	- 2 Waltzes, A flat and E flat. Mazurka, Op. 7: no. 2 (1st version).
Est, Baronne d' - - -	- Polonaise, Op. 22.
Esté, Mme. d' - - -	- Fantasie-Impromptu, Op. 66 (Posth.).
Esterházy, Comtesse - -	- Impromptu, Op. 51.
Flahaut, Comtesse Emilie de	- Bolero, Op. 19.
Fontana, Julian - - -	- 2 Polonaises, Op. 40.
Franchomme, Auguste -	- Sonata for PF. & cello, Op. 65.
Freppa, Mme. Lina - -	- 4 Mazurkas, Op. 17.
Fürstenstein, Comtesse Adèle de	- Scherzo, Op. 31.
Gaillard, Emil - - -	- Mazurka in A minor. Waltz in E flat (?).
Gavard, Elise - - -	- Berceuse, Op. 57.
Gladkowska, Konstancja -	- Waltz, Op. 70: no. 3.
Gutman, Adolf - - -	- Scherzo, Op. 39.

Hanka, Vaclav - - - - Mazurka in G major.
Hartmann, Caroline - - - Rondo, Op. 16.
Hiller, Ferdinand - - - 3 Nocturnes, Op. 15.
Hoffmann, Klementyna - - Mazurka, Op. 67: no. 3.
Horsford, Emma - - - *Ludovic* Variations, Op. 12.
Horsford, Laura - - - Waltz, Op. 18.
Ivri, Baronne C. d' - - - Waltz, Op. 34: no. 2.
Jerzejewicz, Louise (*née* Chopin) - 'Lento con gran espressione' (?).
Johns, M. - - - - - 5 Mazurkas, Op. 7.
Kalkbrenner, Friedrich - - Concerto, Op. 11.
Kessler, Joseph Christoph - - Preludes, Op. 28. (German Edition).
Kolberg, Wilhelm - - - Mazurka, Op. 7: no. 4. Polonaise in
                                B flat minor.
Könneritz, Mlle. R. de - - 2 Nocturnes, Op. 62.
Léo, Auguste - - - - Polonaise, Op. 53.
Linde, Mme. - - - - Rondo, Op. 1.
Liszt - - - - - - Studies, Op. 10.
Lobau, Comtesse Caroline de - Impromptu, Op. 29.
Maberly, Mlle. Catherine - - 3 Mazurkas, Op. 56.
Merk, Josef - - - - Polonaise, Op. 3.
Mlokosiewicz, Mlle. - - - Mazurka, Op. 67: no. 1.
Moriolles, Comtesse A. de - - Rondo à la Mazur, Op. 5.
Mostowska, Comtesse Rosa - 4 Mazurkas, Op. 33.
Müller, Friederike - - - 'Allegro de Concert', Op. 46.
Noailles, Pauline de - - - Ballade, Op. 47.
Perthuis, Comte de - - - 4 Mazurkas, Op. 24.
Perthuis, Comtesse E. de - - Sonata, Op. 58.
Pixis, Johann Peter - - - Fantasia on Polish Airs, Op. 13.
Plater, Comtesse Pauline - - 4 Mazurkas, Op. 6.
Pleyel, Camille - - - - Preludes, Op. 28 (French Edition).
Pleyel, Marie - - - - 3 Nocturnes, Op. 9.
Potocka, Comtesse Delphine - Concerto, Op. 21. Waltz, Op. 64:
                                no. 1.
Radziwill, Prince Antoine - - PF. Trio, Op. 8.
Rothschild, Baronne C. de - - Ballade, Op. 52. Waltz, Op. 64:
                                no. 2.
Schumann - - - - Ballade, Op. 38.
Skarbek, Comte Michel - - Polonaise, Op. 71: no. 1.
Skarbek, Comtesse Viktoire - Polonaise in G minor.
Souzzo, Princesse Catherine de - Fantasia, Op. 49.
Sowińska, Katarina - - - 'Schweizerbub' Variations.
Stirling, Jane - - - - 2 Nocturnes, Op. 55.
Stockhausen, Baron de - - Ballade, Op. 23.

Stockhausen, Baronne de -	- Barcarolle, Op. 60.
Szeremetieff, Anna - -	- *Moderato* in E major.
Szmitowski, Leon - -	- 3 Mazurkas, Op. 50.
Szymanowska, Celina -	- Mazurka in A flat.
Thun-Hohenstein, Mlle. de	- Waltz, Op. 34: no. 1.
Veyret, Mme. A - -	- Polonaise-Fantasia, Op. 61.
Witwicki, Stefan - -	- 4 Mazurkas, Op. 41.
Wodzińska, Maria - -	- Waltz, Op. 69: no. 1.
Wolff, Pierre - - -	- Prelude in A flat.
Wolowska, Alexandra -	- Mazurka in B flat.
Woyciechowski, Titus -	- Variations, PF. Duet (Lost). Variations, Op. 2. [Chopin intended Op. 40: no. 1 to be dedicated to Woyciechowski.]
Württemberg, Princesse de	- 4 Mazurkas, Op. 30.
Żwyny, Wojciech - -	- Polonaise in A flat.

Appendix VI

THE POETS OF CHOPIN'S SONGS

1. Count Zygmunt Kraskiński (1812–1859): poet of mystic patriotism and friend of Mickiewicz. His poems include the 'Undivine Comedy', the 'Psalm of Life' and the drama *Irydion*.
   Author of the song: 'Melodya' (**165**).

2. Adam Bernard Mickiewicz (1798–1855): Poland's greatest poet-patriot. Author of *The Ancestors*, *Crimean Sonnets*, *Konrad Wallenrod* and of the poem 'Świteź' on which Chopin's Ballade, Op. 38 (**102**) is supposed to be based. In July 1834 Mickiewicz married Celina Szymanowska, daughter of Maria Szymanowska. He resided intermittently in Paris from 1832 onwards. He was at one time Professeur au Collège de France, and became acquainted with Chopin, who played the piano at his home *c*. 1835.
   Author of the songs: 'Precz z moich oczu!' (**48**),
   　　　　　　　　　　　'Moja pieszczotka' (**112**).

3. Wincenty Pol (1809–1876): a soldier-poet and patriot. His chief poem is 'The Song of our Land'—a description in verse of districts in Poland.
   Author of the song: 'Śpiew grobowy' (**101**).

4. Stefan Witwicki (1800–1847): a lyric poet but a minor figure in Polish literature. A friend of Mickiewicz in Paris for a short time, but the two quarrelled over political matters. Witwicki enjoyed a closer acquaintance with Chopin than any other of the associated poets. He died of a spinal disease in Rome.
   Author of the songs:

'Życzenie' (**33**)	'Czary' (**51**)
'Gdzie lubi' (**32**)	'Smutna Rzeka' (**63**)
'Wojak' (**47**)	'Narzeczony' (**63**)
'Hulanka' (**50**)	'Piosńka Litewska' (**63**)
'Posel' (**50**)	'Pierścień' (**103**)
'Wiosna' (**116**)	

5. Josef Bohdan Zaleski (1802–1886): called the Ukrainian Nightingale by Mickiewicz with whom he enjoyed a close friendship in Paris in the 1830's. His poetry 'has the wild charm, the mystic music, of the Steppes'. His most famous poem is called 'The Spirit of the Steppe'.
   Author of the songs:

'Śliczny chłopiec' (**143**)	'Dwojaki koniec' (**156**)
'Dumka' (**132**)	'Nie ma czego trzeba' (**156**).

Appendix VII

CHOPIN'S ADDRESSES IN PARIS

August 1831 to end of 1832: Boulevard Poissonnière 27.
1833: Cité Bergère 4.
End of 1833 to September 1836: Rue de Montblanc 5 ⎫
                                Rue de la Chaussée d'Anton ⎭
                                The same house, with a double address.
October 1836 to November 1838: Rue de la Chaussée d'Anton 38.
    [Majorca]
October 1839 to Summer 1841: Rue Tronchet 5.
October 1841 to October 1842: Rue Pigalle 16.
October 1842 to June 1849: Cité d'Orléans.
                                Place d'Orléans 9 ⎫
                                Rue St. Lazare 34 ⎭
                                The same house, with a double address.
June 1849 to September 1849: Grande rue 74, Chaillot.
September 1849 to October 1849: Place Vendôme 12.

Appendix VIII

THREE AUTOGRAPH ALBUMS

1. Emily Elsner (before 1830):
   Waltz in A flat (**21**), Waltz in E flat (**46**), Mazurka, Op. 7: no. 2 (**45**).
   Seven songs: 'Gdzie lubi' (**32**), 'Życzenie' (**33**), 'Wojak' (**47**).
        'Precz z moich oczu!' (**48**), 'Hulanka' (**50**), 'Posel'
        (**50**), 'Czary' (**51**).
2. Maria Wodzińska (1836):
   Nocturne: *Lento con gran espressione*, in C sharp minor (**49**).
   Seven songs: 'Gdzie lubi', 'Wojak', 'Precz z moich oczu!',
        'Hulanka', 'Posel', 'Czary', 'Piosńka Litewska' (**63**).
3. Delphine Potocka (1836–1844):
   Prelude in A major, Op. 28: no. 7 (**100**).
   Two waltzes, published as the 'Deux Valses Mélancholiques'
    (*a*) in B minor (Op. 69: no. 2),
    (*b*) in F minor (Op. 70: no. 2).
   Song: 'Melodya' (**165**).
   This Album also contained a Mazurka in F sharp major, which
   Chopin had copied out for Delphine Potocka, without adding the
   true composer's name. As a result the Vienna music publisher,
   J. P. Gotthard, published the work in 1873, in good faith, as a
   mazurka by Chopin. The mis-attribution was pointed out soon
   afterwards by Ernst Pauer, who, at the same time, gave the rightful
   author's name—Charles Mayer.

Appendix IX

BIBLIOGRAPHY

Polish sub-titles are translated in brackets

Journal of the Frédéric Chopin Institute. Warsaw, 1937.

Catalogues: (*a*) *Exposition: Frédéric Chopin.* Bibliothèque Polonaise, Paris, 1932.

(*b*) *Exposition de Centenaire: Frédéric Chopin.* Paris, 1949.

Correspondence: (*a*) *Chopin's Letters.* Collected by Henry Opieński. Trans. by E. L. Woynich. Knopf, New York, 1931.

(*b*) *Correspondance de Frédéric Chopin.* B. Sydow, with Suzanne and Denise Chainaye. 3 vols. Éditions Richard Masse, Paris. 1956–19—.

*   *   *   *

Binental, Leopold
> *Chopin.* Paris, 1934.
> *Chopin (his creative life and his art).* Warsaw, 1937.
> *Chopin: Dokumente und Erinnerungen aus seiner Heimatland.* Trans. A. Guttry. Leipzig, 1932.

Bory, Robert   *La vie de Chopin par l'image.* Geneva, 1949.

Brońarski, Ludwig
> *Chopin et l'Italie.* Lausanne, 1947.
> *Études sur Chopin.* Lausanne, 1944.

Chainaye, Suzanne and Denise   *Du quoi vivait Chopin?* Paris, 1951.

Chybiński, Adolf   *Fryderyk Chopin.* Warsaw, 1910.

Ganche, Edouard   *Dans le Souvenir de Frédéric Chopin.* Paris, 1925.

Hedley, Arthur   *Chopin.* J. M. Dent & Sons, London, 1947.

Hoesick, Ferdinand   *Chopin (Life and Work).* Warsaw, 1904–1911.

Jachimecki, Zdzisław   *Fryderyk Chopin.* Cracow, 1927.

Karlowicz, Michael   *Souvenirs inédits de Chopin.* Trans. Laure Disiere. Paris, 1904.

Kobylańska, Krystyna   *Chopin in der Heimat.* (German Edition). Polish Music Publishers. Cracow, 1955.

Mirska, Maria   *Szlakiem Chopina.* Warsaw, 1935.

Niecks, Frederick   *Frederick Chopin as a man and musician.* London,
                           1888.
Sydow, Bronisław   {*Bibliografia F. F. Chopina.* Warsaw, 1949.
                           {*Almanach Chopinowski 1949.* Warsaw, 1950.
Szulc, Marcel Antoine   *Fryderyk Chopin (and his compositions).* Poznan,
                           1873.
Weinstock, Herbert   *Chopin.* New York, 1949.
Zagiba, Franz   *Chopin und Wien.* Vienna, 1951.

Indexes

1. WORKS ARRANGED IN CATEGORIES

PIANOFORTE SOLO

Songs, Op. 74

PIANOFORTE DUET (2 PIANOS)

CHAMBER MUSIC

PIANOFORTE AND ORCHESTRA

LOST WORKS

2. WORKS WITH OPUS NUMBERS

3. WORKS WITHOUT OPUS NUMBERS

For nicknamed compositions, and for Wessel's dubbed titles, *see* General Index, under Nicknamed Compositions, and Appendix IV.

General Index

The numbers in this index are item numbers, not page numbers

PRINTED IN GREAT BRITAIN
BY ROBERT MACLEHOSE AND CO. LTD
THE UNIVERSITY PRESS, GLASGOW